Mike Smith's
HOCKEY
PLAYBOOK

REVISED EDITION

FIREFLY BOOKS

A FIREFLY BOOK

Published by Firefly Books Ltd. 2011

First printing

Publisher Cataloging-in-Publication Data (U.S.)

Smith, Michael A., 1945-
    Mike Smith's hockey playbook / Michael A. Smith.
[168] p. : ill. ; cm.
Summary: Step-by-step diagrams and explanations
of strategies for playing ice hockey.

ISBN-13: 978-1-55407-889-9
ISBN-10: 1-55407- 889-X

1. Hockey – Coaching. I. Title.
796.962 dc22   GV848.25.S658 2011

Library and Archives Canada Cataloguing in Publication

Smith, Michael A., 1945-
    Mike Smith's hockey playbook / Michael A. Smith.

Previously published under titles: The hockey play book
and The hockey coach's manual.

ISBN-13: 978-1-55407-889-9
ISBN-10: 1-55407-889-X

1. Hockey – Coaching. I. Title. II. Title: Hockey playbook.
III. Title: Hockey coach's manual.

GV848.25.S655 2011   796.96207'7   C2011-902347-4

Published in the United States by
Firefly Books (U.S.) Inc.
P.O. Box 1338, Ellicott Station
Buffalo, New York 14205

Published in Canada by
Firefly Books Ltd.
66 Leek Crescent
Richmond Hill, Ontario L4B 1H1

Cover and interior design:
Janice McLean /Bookmakers Press Inc.

Cover photo copyright © Ryan McVay/Getty Images

Printed in China

The Publisher gratefully acknowledges the financial support for our publishing program by the Government of Canada through the Canada Book Fund as administered by the Department of Canadian Heritage.

LEGEND

RD   Right Defenseman

LD   Left Defenseman

RW   Right Wing

LW   Left Wing

C   Center

X_1 Right Defenseman

X_2 Left Defenseman

X_3 Right Wing

X_4 Left Wing

X_5 Center

    Pass (arrow shows direction)

    Player movement (arrow shows direction)

    Shot (arrow shows direction)

    Full Stop

    Possession of puck

    Point of contact

△   Pylon

CONTENTS

INTRODUCTION

HOCKEY IS A GAME PLAYED BY YOUNG ATHLETES AND A GAME IN WHICH youth is not entirely determined by age. NHL players bring the same enthusiasm to the rink as eight-year-olds, and no matter what level the players, it is the coach's responsibility to create an atmosphere and environment that gives shape to that enthusiasm. Games are fun. That's why people of all ages play them.

The techniques explained in these pages are cut-and-dried; the diagrams and text are brief and to the point. Coaches reading this book, however, need to remember that their job is to bring these plays to life and that the lessons contained in this book are intended to channel players' excitement, never to stifle it.

This book focuses on the different systems that are part of hockey. There is no one system, no best system, no secret system. Hockey systems are not complex or difficult to learn, although some, it is true, can be challenging to execute. They do take teamwork, though, and it is part of the coach's job—actually, a major part—to foster an eager and effective team spirit and, once that exists, to orchestrate its actions.

When I started coaching in the early 1970s, I thought the road to being a good coach was straight. If I learned A and then B and C, and so on, I would become a skilled coach and know everything I needed to know. But I discovered that the more I learned, the less I knew. What once looked clear and simple often became gray and diffused.

I concluded that a good coach had to become an artist and that the process of guiding a hockey team was subjective. I learned that a good coach must constantly create if he is to enable his players and his team to grow.

The purpose of this book, then, is to provide resources for coaches who are caught up in their own creative efforts. These chapters include different systems for hockey's defensive, offensive and special teams situations. Teaching methods and drills are provided, and the systems run the gamut from the conservative to the aggressive. Some systems are designed specifically for big physical teams or for fast-skating and highly skilled teams or for teams that have both. In this book, there should be a system for every coach.

But here's a warning. Despite the look of this book, hockey is definitely not a game of x's and o's. Diagrams help, but a coach is in trouble if ever he thinks players can learn the game from a chalkboard. It is vital not to make hockey rigid. It is a fast-flowing game with the opportunity for physical confrontation, and it is important for the coach to incorporate both the flow and the physical elements into his plans.

In a sense, the game of hockey resembles jazz. Talents and skills are necessary, but a basic framework is required within which to exercise these abilities. Both jazz and hockey demand improvisation; the individual player doing the extra unexpected bit makes the system work. The individuals play off each other and constantly adjust to one another, and in hockey, just as in jazz, too much planning can ruin everything.

There is no perfect system. Different coaching philosophies emphasize different techniques. Coaches who believe in aggressive, attacking play proceed differently than coaches who believe in a conservative, close-checking approach. Some coaches want aggression in some zones and conservative play in others, and a coach must come to grips with his philosophy of the game before selecting specific systems for play in any one of them.

Once a coach has decided what kind of team he has at his disposal and knows roughly how he wants to proceed, this book can help him lay out his plans. It can help with adjustments to his present techniques and maybe contains a couple of ideas he hasn't thought of before. Later in the season, when the team is in a slump and enthusiasm is slipping away, perhaps this book can even supply a little of the creative magic that every coach should always be looking for.

SKILLS, TACTICS & CONDITIONING

HOCKEY IS A GAME THAT NEEDS GOOD SOUND FUNDAMENTAL SKILLS, skills that become the foundation for both the individual players and the team. Team tactics, for example, cannot be executed without the proper level of skill development. It is essential that coaches learn what skills should be stressed for their team. The fundamental skills must be taught at a pace that permits the individual players to execute them correctly. The desired high-tempo execution of the skills that is sought by and expected of elite teams cannot be attained without proper development of these skills.

A key ingredient to successful coaching is to know what your team is able to do and how to build upon it. While the content of practices should vary for different age groups, there is often a tendency to include drills in a team's practice that are beyond the players' abilities. Coaches need to know what is appropriate.

Teaching team tactics must take a logical path. First, certain tactics are often too complex and difficult for young or poorly skilled teams to execute. Second, some of these tactics must be broken down and taught in parts in order for players to learn them. Introducing tactical skills in this manner allows the complete system to be put together gradually. (The total should be greater than the sum of the parts.) Third, there should be common ground between the players and the tactical system. The players' abilities must fit the system, and the system must complement their abilities.

It is important for the coach to have an understanding of the physiological guidelines of skill development. The physical development determines the level of conditioning for each age group. The players need to have reached the necessary developmental levels prior to the introduction of certain conditioning techniques. What may be good for a team of 15- or 16-year-olds may not be good for other age groups.

AGE BREAKDOWN: This chapter uses three age groups, with each subdivided into two more groups. The young group is 11 and under, the middle group is 12 to 15 years of age, and the older group is 16 and over. The determining factor in these group distinctions is physical development. The young group is prepuberty, the middle group is going through and just completing puberty, and the older group is approaching physical maturity.

The book uses the following age breakdown:

Young Group:	9 and under	10 and 11
Middle Group:	12 and 13	14 and 15
Older Group:	16 and 17	18 and over

The young age group's training is quite basic. All the skills, such as skating, passing, shooting and puckhandling, should be introduced by the age of 11. These drills, however, should be taught patiently with simple and direct drills. With regard to tactics, this age group should become familiar with the rink areas—slot area, deep zones, blue-line area and along the boards. "Rink sense" reflects a knowledge of the different areas. Even these young players should learn why the areas are important, how the areas contribute to the game, and they should be developing a feel for their responsibilities when they are positioned in them. The conditioning has to be simple. Off-ice drills should include easy running, acrobatics and basic coordination drills. On-ice conditioning drills should cover only the normal skill-development drills.

The middle age group's training is more intricate. The skills should be taught by combining two or more skills when possible. A shooting drill that also utilizes passing and skating, for example, can be implemented. Three aspects of tactical training can be taught to the middle group. First, it is time for the players to learn and apply certain

concepts to their game, such as the difference between offense and defense, attack and counterattack, the importance of being a man-down or a man-up, controlling the slot area and playing the man. Second, they are also ready to learn individual tactics, such as backchecking, a one-man forecheck, a two-man forecheck and man-to-man coverage. Third, it is time to introduce noncomplex team tactics. This age group should demonstrate a growth of "hockey sense," which is a general knowledge and understanding of the game. The conditioning process remains uncomplicated, and off-ice training can feature aerobic runs and general strength development through calisthenics and gymnastics. Coaches should carefully monitor any type of weight training. On-ice conditioning should combine easy short-duration drills along with the general skill-development drills.

The older group's training should be comprehensive. While constantly reteaching the basic skills, coaches should stress the execution of the skills at a high tempo. The individual tactics should be sound. The older group's proficiency with individual tactics should permit the team to learn and execute more complex systems. Off-ice conditioning should introduce strength training using weights. A strong aerobic base should be developed. On-ice conditioning should emphasize a sound anaerobic base, with special attention paid to speed and quickness.

SKILLS

Table 1 lists the degree of concentration for skating, shooting and puck skills.

1. Skill improvement enables the coach to make use of drills that are more advanced in difficulty and tempo.

2. Failure to master the proper skill technique prevents any execution at a high tempo.

3. Do not introduce complex skills to the younger group.

4. The middle group should begin to show a degree of mastering the fundamental skills.

5. The older group, for the most part, should be able to execute most skills at a high or near-high tempo.

TABLE 1. SKILLS

Skills	Young Group 9/under	10-11	Middle Group 12-13	'14-15	Older Group 16-17	18/over
Skating						
Forward	XX	XX	XX	XXX	XXX	XXX
Backward	X	XX	XX	XX	XXX	XXX
Turns	X	XX	XX	XX	XXX	XXX
Spins	X	X	X	XX	XXX	XXX
Jumps		X	XX	XX	XX	XXX
Stops	X	XX	XX	XXX	XXX	XXX
Tumbles and Falls		X	X	XX	XXX	XXX
Sprints		X	XX	XXX	XXX	XXX
Puck Skills						
Dribbling	X	XX	XX	XXX	XXX	XXX
Puck Control	X	XX	XX	XXX	XXX	XXX
Sweep Pass	X	XX	XXX	XXX	XXX	XXX
Snap Pass			X	XX	XXX	XXX
Backhand Pass		X	X	XX	XXX	XXX
Drop and Back Pass		X	X	XX	XX	XXX
One-Touch Pass			X	XX	XX	XXX
Pokecheck		X	X	XX	XXX	XXX
Feet to Stick		X	XX	XX	XXX	XXX
Shooting						
Sweep	X	XX	XX	XXX	XXX	XXX
Snap			X	XX	XXX	XXX
Slap			X	XX	XXX	XXX
Backhand	X	X	XX	XX	XXX	XXX
Rebounds	X	X	XX	XX	XXX	XXX
Tip-Ins/Deflections	X	X	XX	XX	XXX	XXX

The symbol X indicates the suggested age level at which the skill should be introduced. The puck skill "dribbling," for example, should be included in the practices of the youngest group—9 and under. The puck skill "snap pass" should begin with the 12-to-13-year-old group. Wrist and forearm strength is not usually developed until this age. Insufficient strength prevents proper execution of the skill.

The symbol XX indicates the age level at which significant improvement in the execution of the skill should be seen. The skill "backhand shot," for example, while introduced to the 9-and-under group, should improve with the 12-to-13-year-old group.

The symbol XXX indicates the age level at which the skill should be used proficiently. This means the skill should be executed at a high or near-high tempo. This is totally dependent on the skills being properly taught and learned at an early age.

SKILL DRILLS

There should be a progression of skill drills from the stage of introduction to high-tempo execution. In general, coaches should advance their players to the more complex drills only after the basic drill—Drill 1, in this example—is executed at a high level of proficiency. Drills 1, 2 and 3 provide an example of progression in both difficulty and pace.

KEY POINTS

1. Drill 1 can be used by all age groups. The tempo or speed of execution should increase with the age groups.

2. Drill 2 can be used by the middle and older age groups and should increase in tempo with age.

3. Drill 3, if executed at a high tempo, can be used by the older groups and possibly advanced middle groups.

PUCKHANDLING AND TURNS.

Purpose: To introduce turns while handling the puck.

Description: Performed by skating along the two blue lines and the red lines. Obstacles are used as guides.

Tempo: Drill is executed from slow to half speed.

Participation: The entire team with one player following right after another.

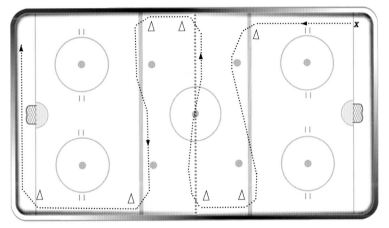

Drill 1 is a simple one that has the players carry a puck around the rink, with pylons for direction. The drill provides plenty of room to maneuver. The turns are neither difficult nor sharp. The speed of the drill is moderate, which gives the players time to concentrate on handling the puck. This is a good drill to introduce the puck skill dribbling to any age group.

PUCKHANDLING AND CIRCLES. **2**

Purpose: To emphasize handling the puck while executing crossovers.

Description: Players skate around each of the five face-off circles. This enables the players to practice crossovers to the left and right while handling the puck.

Tempo: Drill is executed from half to full speed.

Participation: Team is divided into groups of three to five players. The second group starts when the first group has completed its crossovers at the second face-off circle.

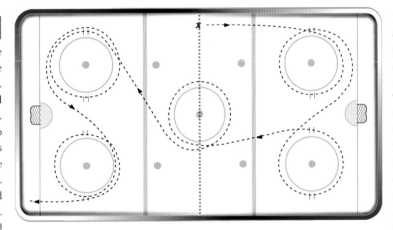

Drill 2 is more difficult. It combines crossover skating with puckhandling. The players skate around each face-off circle while stickhandling with the puck. The speed of the drill ranges from moderate to high tempo. Crossovers and dribbling need to be developed if this drill is to be executed properly. The coach must control the speed to ensure proper execution of the skills. Introduce the drill by having the player skate crossovers while stickhandling without the puck. Good for middle age groups that have shown improvement in the two skills.

PUCKHANDLING AND STOPS. **3**

Purpose: To emphasize puckhandling at a high tempo.

Description: Players skate the length of the ice executing turns and stops at the blue and red lines. Use pylons as guides.

Tempo: Executed at full speed.

Participation: The team is divided into groups of three. The second group leaves after the first group passes the near blue line.

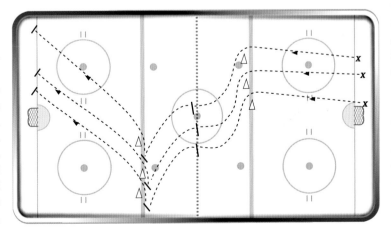

Drill 3 combines the skills of skating forward, stops and puckhandling. To be effective, the drill should be executed at full speed. Players need to make strong stops and quick starts and handle the puck while skating fast and showing good technique. Poor technique will force the players to lose the puck or to do the drill at a slower speed.

INDIVIDUAL TACTICS

Table 2 lists the individual tactics. There are two kinds of tactics: individual and team. Players must learn individual tactics prior to team tactics. Success at team tactics depends on the development of individual skills and individual tactics. The forechecking situation of 1-on-1 is an individual tactic. The 1-2-2 is a team tactic. The 1-on-1 forechecking situation is utilized, however, in the 1-2-2. Thus, it is critical that the players be able to execute the 1-on-1 situation if the 1-2-2 system is to be effective.

KEY POINTS

1. Most individual tactics should be introduced by 10 to 11 years of age.

2. Most tactics are not executed at a high tempo until 16 to 17 years of age.

3. Generally, individual tactics coincide with the development of skills and with increasing understanding of the game.

TABLE 2. INDIVIDUAL TACTICS

	Young Group		Middle Group		Older Group	
	9/under	10-11	12-13	14-15	16-17	18/over
Skills						
Forecheck						
1-on-1	X	X	XX	XXX	XXX	XXX
1st Man/2nd Man		X	X	XX	XXX	XXX
5-Man			X	XX	XXX	XXX
Backcheck						
Man-to-Man	X	X	XX	XXX	XXX	XXX
Open Man			X	XX	XXX	XXX
Team Coverage		X	X	XX	XXX	XXX
Breakouts						
Positional	X	X	XX	XXX	XXX	XXX
One-Man Passes		X	XX	XXX	XXX	XXX
5-Man		X	XX	XX	XXX	XXX
Move to Open Space		X	X	XX	XXX	XXX
Screening			X	XX	XXX	XXX

The symbol X indicates the suggested age level at which to begin teaching the tactic.

The symbol XX indicates the age level at which significant improvement should be made in executing the tactic.

The symbol XXX indicates the age level at which the tactic should be executed at a high tempo.

TACTICAL DRILLS

There should be a progression of individual tactical drills from introduction to high-tempo execution. Forechecking drills 1, 2 and 3 provide examples for such a pattern.

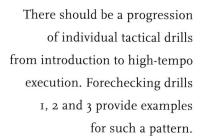

KEY POINTS

1. Drill 1 is a basic individual forechecking drill. It is an excellent drill to teach 1-on-1 forechecking. It can be used by all age groups, including the youngest.

2. Drill 2 is an excellent introductory one for 2-on-1 forechecking. It can be used by the middle and older groups and possibly by the 10-to-11-year-olds.

3. Drill 3 teaches the more advanced 2-on-1 forecheck. It can be used by the older groups and the middle groups if they have mastered the individual tactics taught in Drills 1 and 2.

Forechecking.
1
Purpose: To teach the forwards to check the puck carrier (1-on-1).
Description: An offensive player (O1) carries the puck behind the goal line. The checking forward X1 skates parallel to O1, staying a half-stride behind while maintaining the same speed. X1 forces O1 to go behind the net, prevents him from cutting up the middle and is in a position to skate O1 into the boards and to maintain physical control.
Participation: Two players. Can be executed at both ends.

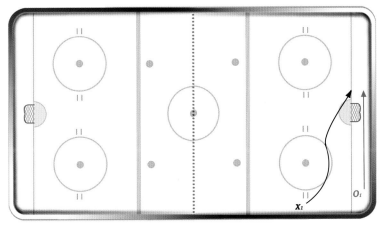

Drill 1 simply teaches the player to forecheck the puck carrier in a 1-on-1 situation. This drill enables the player to utilize both the boards and the net for assistance. The speed of the drill is slow to high tempo, with the younger groups using the slower speeds. The drill teaches how to play the man and not allow the puck carrier to get around or to cut behind the checker.

Forechecking.
2
Purpose: To teach two forwards to pressure the puck carrier 2-on-1.
Description: The puck carrier (O1) starts a few feet ahead of the first forechecker (X1). X1 forces O1 to the boards. The second forechecker (X2) moves in from a different direction. The first forechecker should play the man, and the second takes the puck.
Participation: Three players. Can be executed at both ends.

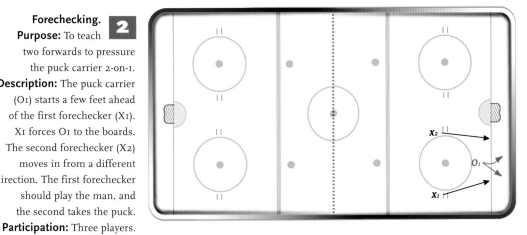

Drill 2 is a more difficult one. It teaches forechecking the puck carrier in a 2-on-1 situation. It calls for the two checkers (X1 and X2) to work in tandem. It is important for the players to work together; otherwise, the puck carrier (O1) will be able either to carry the puck or to pass it. The speed of this drill is moderate to high tempo. What is learned in Drill 1 about 1-on-1 forechecking is essential for this drill to be useful.

Forechecking.
3
Purpose: To teach the center and puck-side wing to forecheck in tandem in the neutral zone.
Description: An offensive player (O1) moves up the ice with the puck. The center (X2) pressures O1 toward the puckside wing (X1), who can then double-team the puck carrier. X1 and X2 can also practice interchanging, with the center going to the boards and the wing pressuring O1.
Participation: Three players.

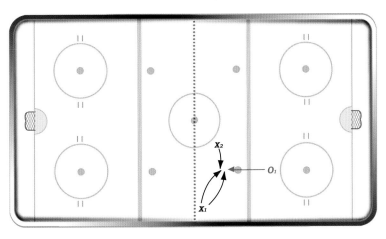

Drill 3 is a high-tempo game-situation drill. It teaches 2-on-1 forechecking in the neutral zone. The two forecheckers (X1 and X2) must check the puck carrier (O1) in the open ice. They do not have the net or the boards to assist them. What is learned in Drills 1 and 2 is essential for this drill.

TEAM TACTICS

Table 3 lists the developmental progress for team tactics that coaches can expect from their players and indicates that the conservative systems are normally introduced to the 10-to-11 and 12-to-13-year-old groups.

Puck-control systems, which generally combine conservative and aggressive elements, are introduced primarily at the 12-to-13-year-old level, when most players develop sufficient skills to utilize such systems. Puck-control systems are not emphasized until players reach the 14-to-15-year-old group, when they are able to handle this type of system. Aggressive systems, on the other hand, are not introduced until the 14-to-15-year-old group. The older groups should be able to execute nearly all the systems at the high-tempo level.

KEY POINTS

1. Systems and tactics are totally dependent on the skill levels of the individual players.

2. Team tactics are, for the most part, taught only in a limited sense to the younger groups. The youngest group, 9 and under, for example, is not normally developed enough to warrant use of hockey systems.

TABLE 3. TEAM TACTICS

Tactic	Young Group 9/under	10-11	Middle Group 12-13	14-15	Older Group 16-17	18/over
Forechecking						
1	X	X	XX	XXX	XXX	XXX
2			X	XX	XXX	XXX
3				X	XX	XXX
Breakouts						
1	X	X	XX	XXX	XXX	XXX
2			X	XX	XXX	XXX
3				X	XX	XXX
Center Ice						
1			X	XXX	XXX	XXX
2			X	XX	XXX	XXX
3				X	XX	XXX
Offensive Zone						
1		X	XX	XXX	XXX	XXX
2			X	XX	XXX	XXX
3				X	XX	XXX
Defensive Coverage						
1		X	XX	XXX	XXX	XXX
2			X	XX	XXX	XXX
3				X	XX	XXX
Power Play						
1		X	XX	XXX	XXX	XXX
2			X	XX	XXX	XXX
3			X	XX	XXX	XXX
Penalty Killing						
1		X	XX	XXX	XXX	XXX
2			X	XX	XXX	XXX
3				X	XXX	XXX
Face-Offs	X	X	XX	XX	XXX	XXX

The symbol X indicates the suggested age level at which to begin teaching the tactic.

The symbol XX indicates the age level at which significant improvement should be made in executing the tactic.

The symbol XXX indicates the age level at which the tactic should be executed at a high tempo.

Key:
1 indicates simple basic systems.

2 indicates systems that combine basic with some innovation.

3 indicates aggressive and advanced systems.

CONDITIONING

Table 4 lists the breakdown of the components of conditioning by age. This table simply indicates the recommended age level at which coaches should begin or continue training for the specific components of conditioning.

KEY POINTS

1. The age group 10 to 11 has had a little more than half of the components introduced, while the 9-and-under group has had only five.

2. By age 12 to 13, all skill components have been introduced.

3. The table illustrates that conditioning does not become a major part of a hockey program until the middle age groups. Even then, it is not until the older groups that conditioning receives due emphasis.

TABLE 4. CONDITIONING

The symbol X indicates the age level at which conditioning should begin.

	Young Group		Middle Group		Older Group	
	9/under	10-11	12-13	14-15	16-17	18/over
Motor Skills						
Balance	X	X	X	X	X	X
Agility	X	X	X	X	X	X
Coordination	X	X	X	X	X	X
Speed of Movement	X	X	X	X	X	X
Speed of Reaction		X	X	X	X	X
Power			X	X	X	X
Physical Fitness						
Flexibility	X	X	X	X	X	X
Muscular Endurance			X	X	X	X
Muscular Strength						
Body Weight		X	X	X	X	X
Weight Training				*X	X	X
Aerobic			**X	X	X	X
Anaerobic				X	X	X

* Weight training for this group needs to be monitored carefully.

** Used only in a limited sense.

DEFENSIVE PLAY

HOW A TEAM PLAYS WHEN THE OPPOSITION HAS CONTROL OF THE PUCK is defensive play. As unglamorous as it is to fans and players alike, good defense often determines the winning team in a close contest. All successful teams play defense well, because even on defense, there is always the opportunity to grab the tempo away from the opposition and move onto the offensive.

Two things are important, therefore, when a team plays defense: how it defends against the opposition and how it regains control of the puck. The two elements are closely linked.

The defensive strategy is the team's overall style of defensive play. There are three basic styles: (1) conservative, (2) positional with elements of aggressive play and (3) aggressive. For each distinct strategy, a number of systems fit for each of the three zones—forechecking, neutral zone and defensive zone.

Defensive strategies are important for the coach and team. Each coach must be comfortable with the style of play and specific systems that his team uses. This is one area in which good sound coaching pays off. Defensive play requires hard work and discipline.

Three things are vital to success—conditioning, fundamentals and working together as a team.

John Wooden
They Call Me Coach

FORECHECKING

ORECHECKING IS THE PROCESS OF ATTACKING THE OPPOSITION IN the offensive zone and doing so in a way that leads to disruption, which leads to confusion, which leads to chaos, so that your team gains possession of the puck and scores a goal. Forechecking, in other words, is about getting the puck back.

All teams have to be good at forechecking to be successful. Fortunately, there are many forechecking systems, and no one system is the ultimate. All systems have some degree of flexibility built in, and this means that whatever system a coach chooses, adjustments can be made in preparation for a particular team and even during a game.

The choice of a forechecking system will depend on the coach's philosophy and on the personnel available. Some systems are geared for aggressive, quick-skating teams. Others may fit slower-skating teams that emphasize size and physical play.

An aggressive system, one that relies on the better skating ability of the forechecking team, usually attacks before the opposing players are organized and attempts to prevent them from getting into their positions. A conservative-system attack takes place after the opponents are organized, as they begin to move out of their end, and often at a specific place. Some systems combine the aggressive and conservative philosophies.

Every team should master at least one forechecking system and be able to make changes within that system to address different situations. A conservative emphasis works best to protect a lead; a more aggressive approach may be necessary when attempting to come from behind. Knowledge of more than one approach can be beneficial, but a team has to have mastered its primary system before learning a second.

Above all, forechecking demands hard work. Nothing can replace it. As a coach, you are teaching players to create chaos; encourage them by pointing out that contributing to the other team's chaos is a highly satisfying way to expend their energy.

STANDARD TRIANGLE

The triangle stresses one forward on the puck, a second in position to move in to help the first, and the third in position to backcheck or to move to the slot on offense. The defensemen play a normal position. The system attacks the puck and prepares the team for the neutral zone if the offense clears the zone. The system can be used by both quick-skating and physical teams. This is a good system to introduce to young teams. For older teams, it can serve as a starting point for a new season. It teaches players basic checking and rotation as well as how to read and react to each other.

KEY POINTS

1. The Standard Triangle forechecking system is easy to teach, with objectives that are simple and direct.

2. It stresses positional play while permitting interaction between the three forwards.

3. It is adaptable to most breakout plays.

4. It stresses pressuring the puck carrier.

5. The primary defensive principle is to prevent the opposition from breaking out 3-on-2.

6. Its execution requires basic checking techniques.

Basic Alignment.
The three forwards form a triangle in the offensive zone. Either the puck-side wing (LW) or the first forward in the zone attacks the puck. The center backs up the LW, and the third forward (RW) is in the slot. The defensemen (LD and RD) take normal positions.

1

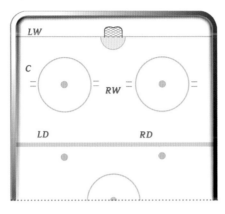

2

The objective is to pressure the puck carrier. The LW moves on X1. The center positions himself either to move in and help the LW or to stay with X3.

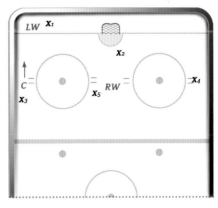

If the LW has two players to contend with (X1 and X5), the center moves in to help. The LD must be in position to check X3.

3

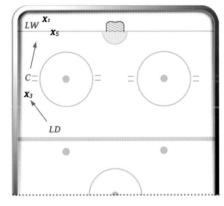

4

If the puck is passed behind the net (X1 to X2), the RW moves in to pressure X2. The center then moves across to back up the RW, and the LW moves to the slot, and the triangle is reestablished.

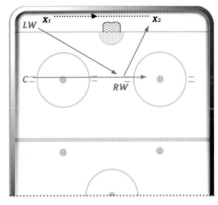

If the puck is passed around the boards to X4, the RD must move in on X4. The LD moves across to cover the RD's position, and the center pulls back to the LD's position.

5

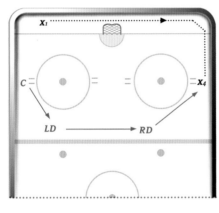

6

This diagram illustrates the triangular positioning of the forwards.

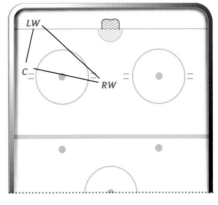

7

This diagram illustrates the triangular configuration, with the center's position backing up the wings.

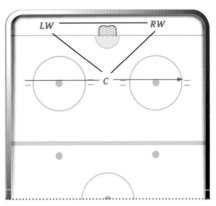

1-2-2

The 1-2-2 is a conservative system designed to prevent 3-on-2 breakouts and to encourage the opposition to set up deep in its own end. It encourages the opposition's defensemen to carry the puck, and it emphasizes control of the boards. One forward, usually the center, forces the puck. The other two forwards, usually the wings, play back near the top of the face-off circles. The defensemen play a normal position. It is a good system for teams with big wingers. It stresses basic checking. All teams, at some time, encounter situations that call for a 1-2-2.

KEY POINTS

1. The 1-2-2 forechecking system is easy to teach, with objectives that are simple and direct.

2. It stresses positional play while permitting basic adjustments and interactions.

3. It is adaptable to most breakout plays.

4. It is positionally balanced: no specific position is the key to the system.

5. It stresses pressuring the puck carrier and checking areas where the puck is likely to go.

6. The primary defensive purpose is to prevent the opposition from breaking out 3-on-2. This is done by keeping both wings back.

7. It is essential for the wings to control the boards.

Basic Alignment. **1**
The center forechecks the puck carrier, the wings (LW and RW) stay wide, checking the opposition's wings, and the defensemen (LD and RD) play inside the wings.

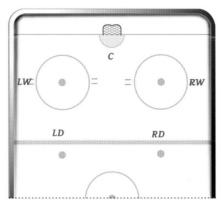

2 The objective of this system is to force the opposition to move the puck to areas covered by the LW and the RW. The center prevents the opposition from moving up the middle. For instance, the center checks X1, the LW has the option of moving in if the center has X1 in check or staying with X3. The LD moves toward the boards and can pinch along the boards. The RD is responsible for the deep middle.

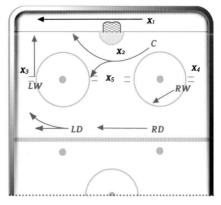

Adjustment to the opposition's breakout. **3** If X5 swings into the corner and X3 comes off the boards straight across the face-off circle, X1 can pass to either X3 or X5. This will flood the area that LW must cover.

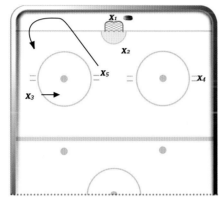

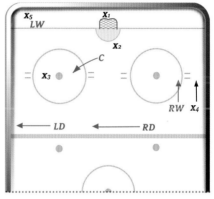

4 The forechecking unit reacts as follows: The LW picks up X5 in the corner before he swings out of the corner. The center moves back and to his left, making it difficult for X1 to pass to X3. The RW keeps X4 in check. The LD moves to the boards, and the RD moves to the middle.

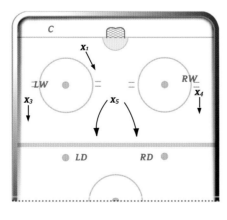

5 If the opposition decides to swing players in both corners, with X2 and X5 swinging into opposite corners, the forechecking unit reacts as follows: The LW picks up X5, the LD picks up X3, the RW picks up X2 in the corner, and the RD picks up X4. The center stays in front of the net to cover X1. The system calls for man-to-man coverage. If anyone fails to cover his man, the forechecking breaks down. If it is successful, X1 will normally have to carry the puck. For the most part, the offensive team will not be as successful clearing the zone with a defenseman carrying the puck as it will with the puck being moved to the forwards.

If the center is beaten, the two **6** wings are in a position to cover the opposition's wings (X3 and X4). This forces the opposition to bring the puck up the middle.

1-4

The 1-4 is a conservative system. One forward, usually the center, pressures the puck. The other two forwards, the wings, play a similar role to that of the defensemen; essentially, four players form a wall across the blue line. The line can move back to the red line as the opposition moves out of the zone. A team often utilizes this system when protecting a lead late in a game. It is frequently used by a team that has significantly less talent. The attack comes as the opposition moves up the ice.

1. The 1-4 forechecking system is easy to teach, with objectives that are simple and direct.

2. It does not stress pressuring the puck carrier in the offensive zone; it essentially gives up the offensive zone.

3. One forward, usually the center, forechecks the puck or forces the opposition to bring the puck up the wing by positioning himself in the middle of the zone.

4. Two forwards, usually the wings, and the two defensemen work as a unit to form a wall across the ice.

5. The four-man unit has a territorial responsibility.

6. The primary defensive principle is to have four players always in position to defend against the opposition's three forwards.

Basic Alignment. **1**
One forward (C) is in the offensive zone. He can either pressure the puck carrier or compel the opposition to go up the boards by shutting off the middle. The other two forwards (LW and RW) form a four-man wall with the defensemen (LD and RD).

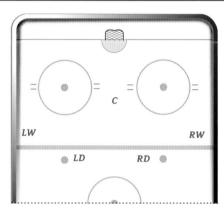

2 *Basic Alignment* when the wall is at the red line. This alignment gives away the offensive zone and sets up the forechecking in the neutral zone.

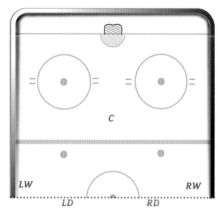

3 The role of the first forward (C) is to control the middle. He can either move in deep on the puck or stay back and shut down the middle.

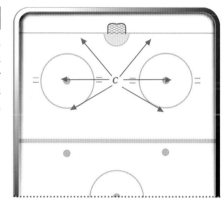

4 The roles for the other four players are basic: The wings cover the boards, and the defensemen cover the middle. Normally, they are not aggressive and do not move deeply into the zone. Rather, their role is to prevent the opposition from advancing the puck through the wall.

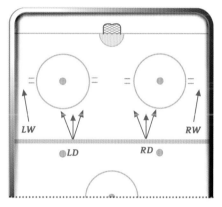

5 The members of the four-man unit react to each other. If the opposition comes up the middle, the LD and the RD play up and the two wings drop back to cover.

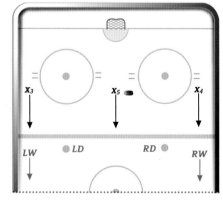

6 If the opposition comes up the boards, one wing and one defenseman (LW and LD) play up and the other two players (RD and RW) drop back to cover.

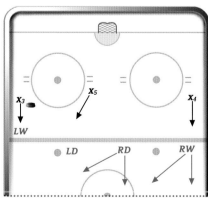

7 When the wall is set up at the red line, the forechecking unit can easily move to the offensive. The wings are in a position to move up quickly, and the center should already be up.

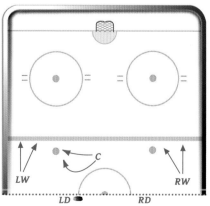

1-1-3 OFF-WING STAY BACK

This system combines aggressiveness with conservatism. The off-side wing always plays back in position to backcheck and defend against 3-on-2 breakouts. The center and puck-side wing have an aggressive responsibility to attack the puck. The defensemen play normal positions. To use this system, teams need to have good skating forwards who can anticipate. When successful, it can result in quick counterattacks on the goal. The conservative forward, the off-side wing, is always in position to move to the slot area.

KEY POINTS

1. The 1-1-3 forechecking system is easy to teach, with objectives that are simple and direct.

2. It combines positional play with controlled movements.

3. It emphasizes aggressive forechecking but reserves one forward in position to assist the defensemen: two forwards, the center and the on-side wing, have aggressive forechecking responsibilities, and the off-side wing has a conservative defensive role.

4. It allows forwards the freedom to be innovative when the occasion arises.

5. This system relies on skating and intense concentration by the forwards.

1 **Basic Alignment.** Two forwards, the center and the puck-side wing (RW), have fore-checking responsibilities. The off-side wing (LW) stays high in the offensive zone. The LW is in a position to move back to play a defensive role or to move to the slot area.

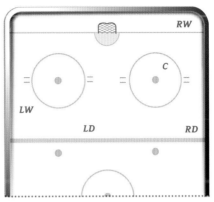

2 The objective is to have the off-side wing (LW) shut down the far board, which forces the opposition to bring the puck up through the forechecking forwards (C and RW). The first forward (RW) fore-checks the puck carrier, and the center is in a position to assist the RW or to move to the puck if the RW is beaten. The RD is permitted to pinch in, and the LD is responsible for the middle.

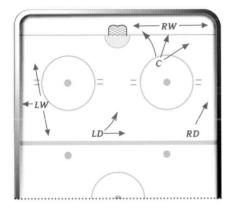

The forwards often have to **3** rotate. As the play moves from one side to the other, the off-side wing (LW) becomes the fore-checker and the puck-side wing (RW) assumes the defensive forward's role. The center's role remains constant.

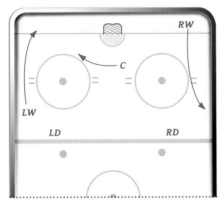

4 Adjustment to the opposition's breakout. If X1 moves to the open area behind the goal line, X2 can pass to him. The objective of this breakout play is to move the puck to an open area (Diagram 5).

The LW checks X3 **5** (LW is too high to move to X2 and would be trapped if he did so). The center moves across the ice, checking X5. The center then has two options: first, to stay with his check (X5), forcing X1 to carry the puck;

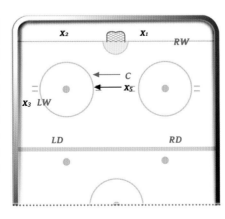

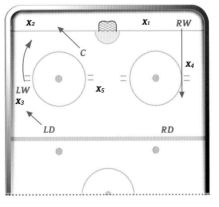

6 or second, to aggressively fore-check X2. If the center executes the second option, the LW moves in as the second forechecker, the LD may pinch along the boards and the RW drops back to assume the role of the defensive forward.

2-3 ONE WING ALWAYS BACK

This system combines aggressiveness with conservatism. Two forwards, a wing and the center, constantly attack the puck. The other wing is in a conservative defensive role, always in position to backcheck and to defend against 3-on-2 breakouts. The defensemen play normal positions. The constant roles of the forwards permit set plays to be executed when counterattacking. This system requires forwards who can skate.

KEY POINTS

1. The 2-3 forechecking system is easy to teach, with objectives that are simple and direct.

2. It combines free, aggressive forechecking by two forwards with a constant defensive role by the third forward.

3. The pressuring forwards have the freedom to be innovative when the occasion arises.

4. This system emphasizes skating, intense concentration and defined roles for the forwards.

Basic Alignment. **1**
Two forwards, the RW and the center, have forechecking responsibilities. The LW always stays high in the offensive zone in a position to become a third defenseman. The defensemen (LD and RD) play shifted toward the right.

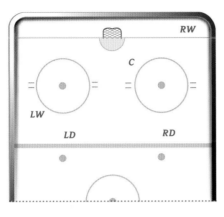

2 The forechecking forwards (RW and C) work in tandem. One forward, usually the first player on the puck, forces the puck. The other forward reacts to the first forward's movements.

When the puck **3**
moves to the LW's side, the LW remains in his defensive position. The center and RW shift their forechecking responsibilities to that side.

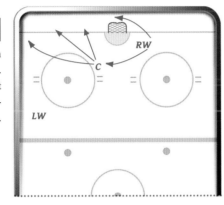

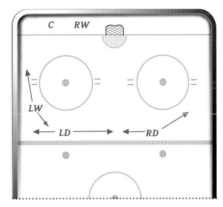

4 With the center and the RW deep, the LW and the RD have the responsibility of defending the boards. They are permitted to pinch if the opportunity arises.

If the RD **5**
pinches along the boards, the LW and the LD must cover for him. The LD moves to play the RD's position, and the LW moves to play the LD's position.

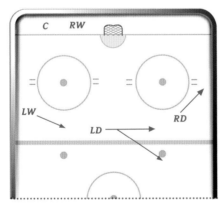

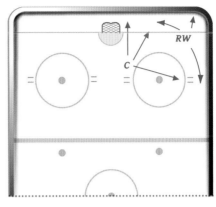

6 The defensive objective of this system is to have three players always in a position to assume defensive roles when the opposition has beaten the two forechecking forwards and has cleared the zone. The LW, LD and RD prevent any 3-on-2 breakouts.

When the forecheckers gain control of the puck, the LW moves **7** to the offense. For example, the RW has the puck, and the LW can move to the slot or deep into the zone. Teams using this system should practice predetermined movements once they gain control of the puck; for example, the RW has the puck, and there are a number of different reactions possible for the other players.

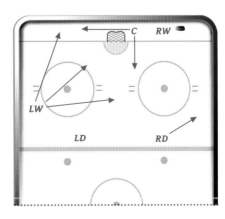

2 - 1 - 2

KEY POINTS

This is an extremely aggressive system, perfected by the Soviet National teams of the 1980s. It calls for constant pressure on the puck by two forwards. Both defensemen play aggressively, pinching in along the boards. This system, when successful, results in the opposition passing the puck either under intense pressure or blindly in their own end. The constant pressure forces quick passes, which can be awkward to execute. This system makes it difficult for an opposition player to carry the puck, since the two forwards will pressure him. This system is *not* for all teams. Constant work, speed and anticipation are essential. This system relies on communication between the center and the defense.

1. The 2-1-2 system is difficult to learn. All the players must thoroughly understand the *defensive* principles.

2. It is a positionally balanced system.

3. It emphasizes the interchanging of positions, which means the players must know the responsibilities of each position.

4. It is a free-flowing system with constant motion, and it emphasizes attacking the opposition at all times and in all areas.

5. It stresses skating and quickness. The ability to play the man is an important asset.

Basic Alignment. **1**
Two forwards (either the wings or the first two forwards) are deep. The third forward (usually the center) plays in the high slot. The two defensemen play wide on the blue line.

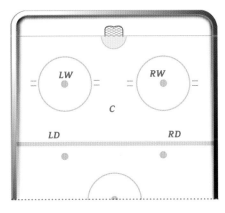

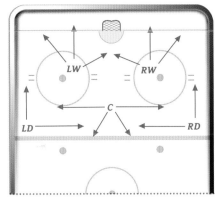

2 The movement of the players permits a great deal of freedom. The structure of the system is symmetrical. The entire zone is covered, with two players always in position to pressure the puck.

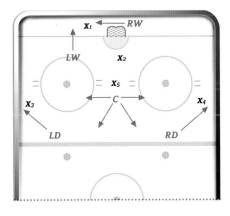

3 The objective is to keep constant pressure on the opposition. The two forecheckers (LW and RW) are aggressive at all times. The third forward (C) backs up the two forecheckers and can become a backchecker or cover for either defenseman, who may pinch along the boards to cover the opposition's wings or the puck. The third forward is also responsible for the middle of the ice and must keep the opposition's center in check.

Adjustment to the opposition's breakout. **4** Constant pressure often forces the opposition to use the boards or to dump the puck to a vacant area. (In this case, the area between the net and the opposite corner is vacant.) If the puck is shot along the boards, the defenseman normally pinches in and the center moves back to cover the blue line. The defenseman's job is to keep the puck deep in the zone. If the puck gets by the defenseman, the center is in position to play defense.

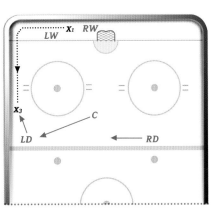

The center has **5** the option of going to the boards if the opposition's wing is deep. The center and the two defensemen must communicate to prevent the center and a defenseman from both pinching in and getting trapped.

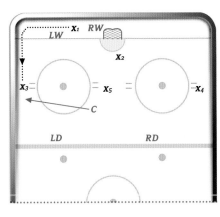

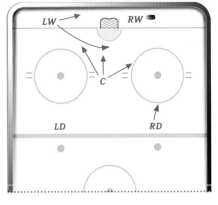

6 If the RW gains control of the puck, the center is in the high slot and can move in deeper or to either side of the slot. The LW can move deep behind the goal line or to the net. The RD can move to the top of the face-off circle.

AGGRESSIVE
2-1-2

This is an aggressive system. It places emphasis on forcing the offensive team toward the boards. This system is structured to box the offensive unit in along the boards. Two forwards, the puck-side wing and the center, are aggressive forecheckers. The two defensemen also have aggressive roles. The off-side wing positions himself either to become a backchecker or to move in and forecheck when the play shifts to his side. This system needs physical forwards.

KEY POINTS

1. The Aggressive 2-1-2 system is easy to teach, with objectives that are simple and direct.

2. It stresses positional play with explicit roles for its players.

3. The aim is to force the offensive team to the boards so that the forechecking unit is then able to apply pressure using the boards as a boundary.

4. Two forwards, the puck-side wing and the center, have aggressive forechecking roles.

5. The role of the off-side wing is to backcheck or to move in and forecheck when the play shifts to his side.

6. The defensemen's roles are aggressive. The puck-side defenseman can pinch along the boards. The other defenseman is responsible for the high slot.

7. Physical play along the boards is important.

Basic Alignment. **1**

The puck-side wing (LW) and the center play deep in the zone. The off-side wing (RW) remains high, close to the top of the face-off circle. The LD plays close to the boards. The RD plays farther to the left than normal.

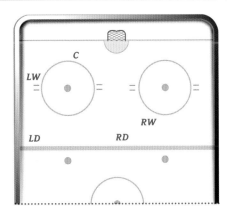

The center (or **2** the LW if he is the first player in the zone) forces the play toward the boards. The LW positions himself to assist the center. The LD can pinch in along the boards when the puck or play is there.

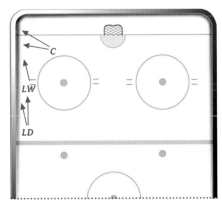

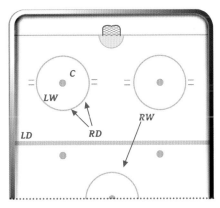

3 The RD's role is to move into the high slot area when the puck or play is there. When the RD moves in, the RW must move back to cover for the RD.

The primary **4** objective of this system is to force the offensive unit to the boards. When this is effective, the offensive team has only one direction to go, directly into the pressure applied by the forechecking unit.

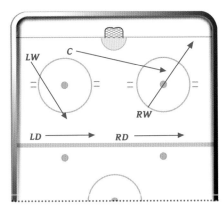

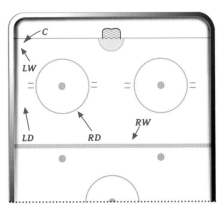

5 The RW is in a position to move quickly to the slot or net area when possession of the puck is gained. For example, if the LW has the puck, the RW moves to the slot and the center moves to the net.

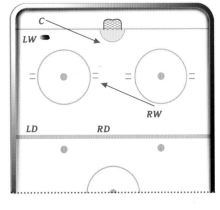

6 When the puck is moved to the opposite corner, the RW moves in to forecheck and the center moves across the ice to help. The LW moves back high to the top of the face-off circle. The defensemen (LD and RD) shift their positions across the blue line.

AGGRESSIVE OVERLOAD

This is an extremely aggressive system. The forwards apply constant pressure. They have no defensive responsibilities; their primary objective is to attack the puck at all times. This system uses both good skating and physical forwards. The defensemen, positioned wider than normal, are permitted to pinch on the puck.

1. The Aggressive Overload system is easy to teach, with objectives that are simple and direct.

2. It is an aggressive system that constantly pressures the puck.

3. The three forwards work together as a unit, and sound interaction between them is essential.

4. The defensemen pinch whenever possible. Their job, when they do pinch, is to get the puck deep into the zone.

5. This system can be effective under specific situations. A small ice surface is useful, but a team trying to overcome a lead may also find it helpful.

6. The pressure comes from exceptional speed or exceptional size; a team with neither should use another system.

Basic Alignment. **1**

The three forwards are in deep (or in the area of the puck). The defensemen play wider than normal on the blue line.

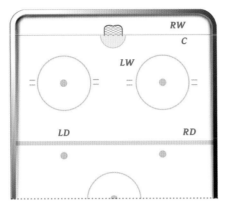

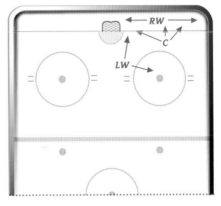

2 The three forwards work together aggressively to pressure the puck. The forwards interact.

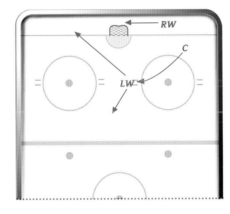

3 One forward should always be higher than the other two. The high forward is in a position to move back, if necessary. Also, the high forward is in position to move to the puck when it moves away from the two deep forwards.

The defensemen are allowed to **4** pinch along the boards. On the puckside, when the RD pinches in, the high forward (LW) moves back toward the blue line.

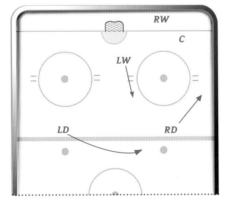

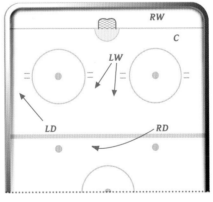

5 When the puck is moved to the far side, the LD pinches in. Again, the high forward (LW) moves back toward the blue line. Depending on his position, the LW will move to either the LD or the RD's position.

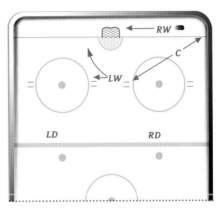

6 When the fore-checking unit gains possession of the puck, the three forwards are already deep and they should apply quick pressure on the net. For example, if the RW has the puck, one or both of the other two forwards (LW and C) should go immediately to the net.

3-2 PRESS

This is a highly aggressive system intended for specific situations: face-offs, end of a period or when a certain (weaker) opponent has the puck. The three forwards attack the puck. It is done with the confidence that the three forecheckers will get the puck and produce a scoring opportunity. The defensemen play a normal position with the freedom to join the pressure close to the blue line. All teams can make use of this system.

KEY POINTS

1. The 3-2 Press system is easy to teach, with objectives that are simple and direct.

2. The primary objective is to have the three forwards pressure the puck simultaneously.

3. This pressure is done with high intensity.

4. The defensemen play a conservative role and remain on the blue line.

5. The forwards apply pressure in an effort to get a quick turnover of the puck and make a direct play on the net.

Basic Alignment. **1**

The three forwards are deep and pressure the puck. The defensemen play a normal position on the blue line.

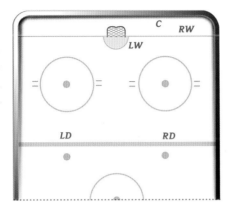

2 Use this system when, for example, X2 (notorious for being poor with the puck) has the puck. Players are instructed ahead of time that when X2 has possession, they are to pressure him in order to create a quick turnover.

After a turnover, **3** the forwards gain possession of the puck and make a quick and direct play on the net.

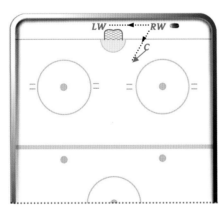

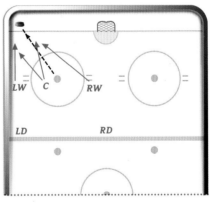

4 A second use for this system is the face-off. The forwards go directly to the puck if the center loses the draw.

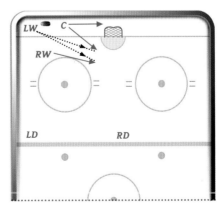

5 Again, a quick and direct play is made on the net after the puck is turned over. The LW has the puck, and the RW and the center move to the net and deep.

DRILLS

The following drills are examples that can be utilized to teach various components of forechecking. Drills can be devised to be specific to the different systems.

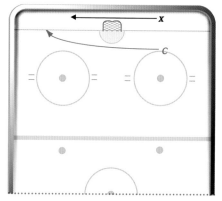

1 Purpose: Teach the forwards to check the puck carrier. An offensive player (X) carries the puck along the boards behind the goal line. The center skates parallel to X, staying a half-stride behind while maintaining the same speed. The center forces X to go behind the net, prevents him from cutting up the middle and is in a position to check X into the boards and to maintain physical control.

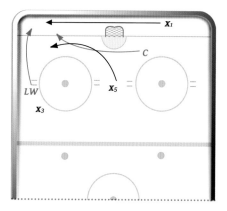

2 Purpose: Practice interaction of the center and a wing. The LW will move in on the puck when the center has X1 in check. If the LW moves too soon, X3 will become open for a pass from X1. A variation is to add X5 and have him swing into the corner. The LW moves in to check X5, and the center moves over to cover X3.

Purpose: Teach the defensemen to pinch and control the boards. The **3** center will move in to check X and force him to shoot the puck along the boards. The defenseman practices moving to the boards and pinching in to keep the puck in play. The puck carrier should vary the type of clearing shot to help the defenseman learn to control the different shots. A variation is to have the defenseman pinch in on a player taking a pass along the boards.

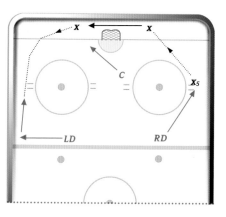

Purpose: Teach the two forecheckers to pressure the puck **4** carrier. The puck carrier (X) starts a few feet ahead of the first forechecker (RW). The RW forces X to the boards and in the direction of the net. The second forechecker (C) moves in from a different direction. The first forechecker takes the man, and the second forechecker takes the puck.

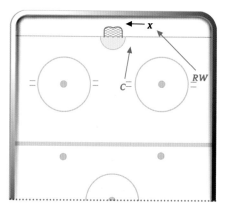

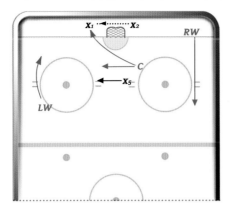

5 **Purpose:** Teach the two forecheckers to react to the opposition's defenseman passing the puck to his partner. The second forechecker (C) reacts to X2's pass to X1 by moving across the ice, keeping X5 in check. The RW pulls back to assume a defensive role. A variation is to have the center forecheck X1 and the LW move in to become the second forechecker.

6 **Purpose:** Teach the interaction of the two defensemen and the off-side wing. The puck carrier (X2) will pass the puck to X4 or shoot the puck along the boards to X4. The RD will either pinch in on X4 or on the puck. The off-side defenseman (LD) moves over to be in position if the play gets by the RD. The off-side wing (LW) moves to the LD's normal position.

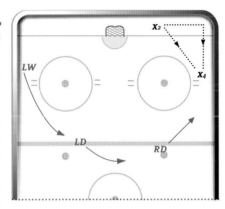

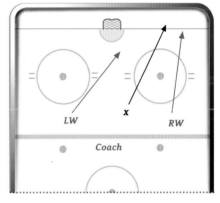

7 **Purpose:** Teach the two forecheckers to press or attack at all times and to work as a unit. The coach dumps the puck into a corner or along the boards. A defenseman (X) retrieves the puck and attempts to make a play. The two forecheckers, starting at different spots, attack X.

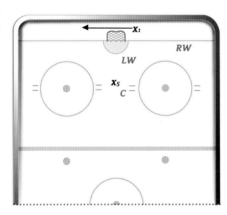

8 **Purpose:** Teach the forwards to interact. Begin with opposition's defenseman (X1) with the puck. Two forecheckers (LW and RW) start 10 feet back. The center must cover X5 to prevent the pass up the middle. Progress to the point that the three forwards interchange positions. Insert a second defenseman (X2) to teach the forecheckers to react to passes between X1 and X2. Often, the center forechecks and one wing assumes the center's position.

9 **Purpose:** Teach the high forward (C) and the two defensemen to interact. This drill has the opposition's defenseman (X1) pass the puck to a wing (X3 or X4). If the wing is high (top of the face-off circle), the defenseman pinches in and the center moves to the blue line. If the wing is deep, the center will move to the wing and the defenseman holds the blue line. Emphasize communication in this drill.

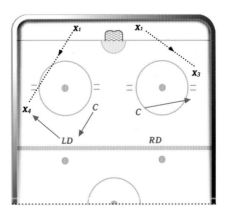

You will not get far using "old skates"—using old tactics, skills and techniques. What was considered the weapon of the strongest yesterday, today becomes accessible to all.

Anatoli Tarasov
The Road to Olympus

NEUTRAL ZONE DEFENSE

DEFENSIVE PLAY IN THE NEUTRAL ZONE IS OFTEN OVERLOOKED, AND too many coaches are content to tell their players just to "stay in your lanes." But neutral zone defense cannot be reactive; defenders will not be effective in the neutral zone if they wait for their opponents to make mistakes. Defenders in the neutral zone must first attack the puck, then actively and consciously oppose the opposition's attempt to get access to its offensive zone.

Fewer defensive systems are available in the neutral zone because the defending team is now being forced back closer to its own goal and the potential consequences of a mistake have increased. With less room on the ice for recovery, there is less room for flexibility. On the other hand, the opportunities to attack the puck are more specific and often obvious, and it is the attack, often referred to as the "trap," that is critical.

The other thing to keep in mind is that successful neutral zone forechecking will lead directly to an effective offense. The counterattack is part of the neutral zone defense, and the transition from defense to offense needs to be deliberate and well practiced so that it can be executed quickly. Skilled neutral zone forechecking will produce a turnover and transition so quick that the offensive unit will be trapped by the change of possession. Drills that practice the counterattack initiated in the neutral zone are a valuable method for teaching the neutral zone forecheck.

One suggestion useful for all systems in the neutral zone is to divide the zone into five "lanes": two outside, two inner and a middle one. The conservative approach has one player responsible for each lane, and the more aggressive systems have flexible or rotating coverage. In either case, the lane approach serves as a spatial reference tool when defining and teaching responsibilities.

The best teacher is repetition, day after day, throughout the season. It must be recognition and instant reaction.

John Wooden
They Call Me Coach

DEFENSIVE ZONE PLAY

GOOD DEFENSIVE ZONE PLAY REQUIRES THAT SIX PLAYERS ACCEPT THE responsibility and execute as a unit to prevent the opposition from scoring and to regain possession of the puck. Each individual must accept his place within the unit and execute his role.

The defensive team goes from attacking to defending in this zone, and the mood changes. More is at stake. The opposition is closer to scoring. There is less playfulness involved because the defensive team has less room for improvisation. Essentially, this zone calls for the basics. Fewer systems are available to a team when it is defending than when it is attacking the puck, and there is less room for errors: a mistake in the defensive zone is likely to result in a direct play on the net.

There are a number of key requirements that apply to all defensive systems:

1. Players must understand the system. Everyone must know each other's responsibilities as well as his own. If one player is beaten, the others must be able to adapt quickly.

2. When checking a player, always stay between the man and the net.

3. When playing the body, do it legally. Effective physical play is accomplished through proper positioning, not through holding, hooking, tripping, etc.

4. Accept the defensive responsibilities as an essential part of the game, equal to or even more important than the other parts.

Defensive play is fundamentally brief. The concepts are simple and direct. Yet the desire to defend is an intangible, and the coach needs to instill positive methods so that players will enjoy this part of the game. "This is what we're doing. This is what needs to be done. This will work."

The coach also needs to emphasize skills that are important to defensive zone play. Some examples are:

split vision—the ability to watch your man and/or zone and the play around the puck; *skating agility*—the ability to move in short distances forward, backward and laterally;

body confidence—the ability to use balance, strength and power to defend in small areas.

ZONE DEFENSE

The Zone Defense is a conservative one. The defensive zone is divided into five sections, one for each player. The system calls for strict positional play, with limited freedom for players to be innovative. It asks the defensive players to outplay their offensive counterparts in all 1-on-1 situations. This system is used by all teams in certain situations. Young teams and those with limited skating ability find this system useful. It is a good system to teach individual players defensive coverage.

KEY POINTS

1. Zone Defense is a basic system that is easy to teach. It does not allow for much adaptation or innovation.

2. It stresses strict defensive coverage, with each player responsible for a given area of the ice surface.

3. It is a balanced defense, with the defensive zone divided into five zones.

4. It allows some overlapping of the zones.

5. The major weakness is that in a mobile game, it is easy for the offense to flood one zone with two or three players, creating a 2-on-1 or 3-on-1 situation.

Basic Alignment.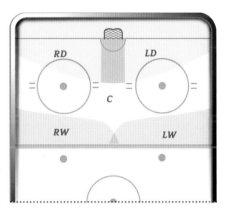
The defensive zone is divided into five zones. There is some overlapping of the zones. The wings cover the two points, the center covers the slot area, and the defensemen cover from the front of the net to the corners.

The objective is to defend against the opposition by covering the entire defensive zone. In a normal situation, one defensive player should be able to play the man or the puck in his zone. For example, if the opposition has the puck in the corner, the puck-side defenseman (RD) will play him. The other defenseman (LD) is in front of the net. The center covers from the slot to the boards. The wings cover their respective points, maintaining a position between the puck and the point.

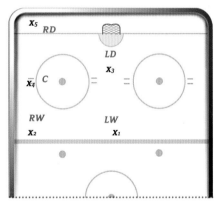

COMBINATION ZONE AND MAN-TO-MAN

This system, called the Combination, includes both conservative and aggressive approaches to defense. A sound understanding of the system's defensive principle is needed by all the players. The defensive zone is divided into five sections, each player responsible for one section; that's the conservative aspect. The players are then also given the freedom to adapt when one zone is flooded and its defensive player is outmanned. This allows the players to pressure the puck, the aggressive aspect. It is a good system for teaching the players to read and react. A team prerequisite is to have a good level of skating ability. Teams with physical players also find this system useful.

KEY POINTS

1. The Combination Zone and Man-to-Man system is easy to teach, with straightforward objectives.

2. It stresses defending the different zones and taking into account the opposition's ability to flood the zones.

3. It encourages a measure of flexibility and innovation.

4. It depends on each player's ability to check successfully in 1-on-1 situations. It permits the players to leave their zones when another zone is flooded. This system does not want 2-on-1 situations to occur.

5. The major weakness is that discipline can be lost. Some players will have a tendency to run around, or "chase the puck," and leave their zones uncovered.

Basic Alignment. Each player has a zone for which he is responsible. **1** (See Zone Defense Diagram 1, page 55.) In addition to the zone, each player is responsible for one opponent. The wings cover the opposition's defensemen, the center covers the opposition's center, and the defensemen cover the opposition's wings. The man-to-man coverage encourages more overlapping of the zones than in the strict Zone Defense.

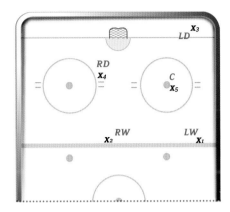

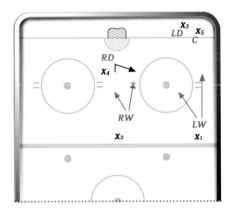

2 The objective is to prevent the opposition from creating any 2-on-1, 3-on-1 or 3-on-2 situations. When the opposition overloads one zone, a defensive player leaves his zone to cover his check. When this happens, the other players increase their zone areas. For example, if the center goes to the corner to help the LD and to cover his check, the center's zone (slot area) is vacated. The RW and the LW become responsible for the high slot, and the RD for the deep slot.

When the play moves into the defensive zone, the **3** wings normally go deep with their checks until the defensemen are able to assume their man-to-man responsibility. The center normally moves to the slot area and covers the trailer, or if one of his wings has gone deep backchecking, the center picks up the wing's responsibilities at the point.

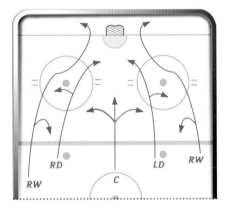

BOX PLUS ONE

The Box Plus One is an aggressive system of defense. It is a balanced system, with the two wings and defensemen forming a box. The system's basic principle is to keep the offensive unit outside the box. The center's role is to assist the other players, especially the defensemen. The center prevents a defenseman from being caught in a 2-on-1 situation and allows the other players to be aggressive and attack the puck. The balance of the system permits the defensive team to attack the puck at every position. This advanced system is not suited to young teams or to those with poor skating ability.

KEY POINTS

1. The Box Plus One is an easy system to teach, with objectives that combine positional and man-to-man play.

2. It is similar to a penalty-killing situation, with the two defensemen and two wings forming a box.

3. The center plays as a third defenseman, and he can also assist the wings.

4. It stresses shutting down the slot, often having two men in position to cover the slot.

5. It is flexible and can adapt to most offenses. It never asks a defensive player to check two men.

6. The opposition defenseman will often be forced to move to the slot area in an attempt to break up the box.

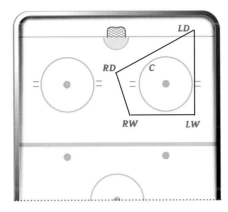

1 **Basic Alignment.** The defensive unit forms a box similar to a four-man penalty-killing formation. The puck-side defenseman (LD) plays the puck, and the other defenseman (RD) guards the front of the net. The puck-side wing (LW) covers his point closely, and the other wing (RW) is responsible for the high slot and the other point. The center normally plays deep as a third defenseman.

The objective is to keep the opposing team outside the box. The center prevents the opposition from creating any 2-on-1 situations.

2

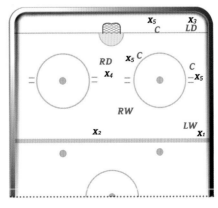

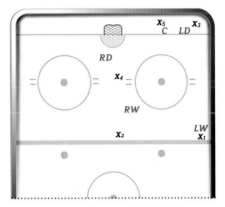

3 The wings have a multipurpose role. The puck-side wing (LW) plays his point tight. He can move in toward the face-off circle if the need arises; however, his main job is to cover the point. The off-side wing (RW) plays in the high slot. This allows the center to be more aggressive and not to be as concerned with the slot. The puck has to go through the high slot to reach the point. The off-side wing is in a position to quickly cover the point.

The center is crucial. His pattern of movement resembles the spokes in a wheel. He never swings through the zone but moves back and forth in straight lines. He plays, primarily, as a third defenseman complementing the others.

4

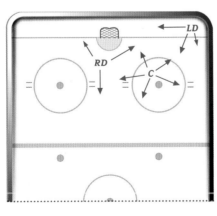

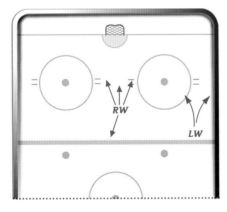

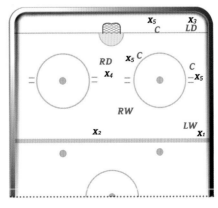

5 The center must come back deep and concentrate on defense. If a second attacking forward is in the corner, the center moves to the corner. If a second attacking forward goes to the net area, the center must play the net area.

59

DRILLS

The following drills are examples that can be utilized to teach coverage in the defensive zone. Remember: Breakouts, clearing the zone with possession of the puck, are part of defensive zone play.

1 **Purpose:** Explain the defensive system, e.g., Zone. The coach goes through each position, describing the responsibilities of each player. The players should be familiar with each position, and the coach must *show* each player his turf. Defensemen: Responsible for area from far goal post to corner and out to the face-off dot. Center: Responsible for slot area from board to board. He has the largest area to cover. Wings: Responsible for area from blue line to top of face-off circle. The wings also have a man-to-man responsibility: they must attempt to limit the opposing defensemen's handling and shooting of the puck.

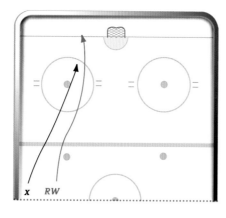

2 **Purpose:** Teach the wings proper backchecking technique. The drill is executed by having an offensive player (X) skate up the ice without the puck. The backchecking wing (RW) stays with X, keeping the following in mind:

1) He stays between X and the puck;
2) He stays within a stick's length of X to prevent him from breaking to the inside;
3) He must be aware of what is happening with the puck (repeatedly looks in direction of the puck);
4) He takes X to the goal post or to the corner;
5) He must exert total control over X, enabling the other players to concentrate on their jobs.

Purpose: Teach the **3** defenseman to play the man. The drill is executed by having an offensive player (X) attempt to skate out of the corner with the puck. The defenseman (RD) plays the man by keeping X to the outside and keeping himself between the puck and the net. The RD plays the man, thus separating X from the puck. An option is to add the center to the drill. He moves in on the puck after the RD has taken control over X.

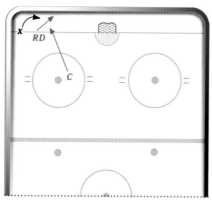

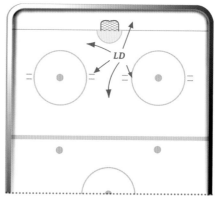

4 **Purpose:** Teach the defensemen proper position in front of the net. The off-side defenseman (LD) lines up on the far goal post. This permits him to view the entire puck-side area and not allow anyone to get behind him to the net. This positioning allows the LD to move to the opposition or the puck.

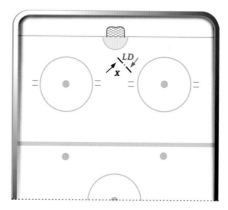

5 **Purpose:** This drill should also have the LD practice picking up an offensive player (X) and keeping him from the front of the net. There is no action to this drill. Nevertheless, it is essential to show defensemen their position.

Purpose: Teach the **6** center to defend the slot area. The center stays with an offensive player (X5) in the slot area. A second offensive player (X4) is in the corner with the puck. A defenseman (RD) plays X4. X4 attempts to pass to X5, and the center must keep X5 in check. An option is to have the center move in on the puck if the RD takes X4 off it.

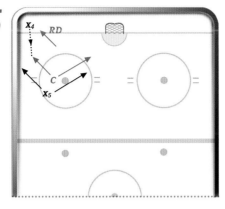

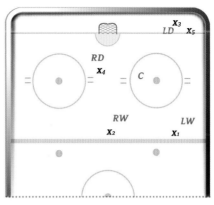

Purpose: Teach **7** gamelike situations. This drill uses complete offensive and defensive units. The coach sets the players in any number of situations. The offense has the puck, and on the whistle, the defense adjusts to the offense in short (7-to-12-second) scrimmages. This drill familiarizes the players with their responsibilities for "Box Plus One." For example, in this setup, the LD is outmanned. On the whistle, the center moves in to help the LD, and the RW moves in to the slot to help the RD cover the center's slot area.

Purpose: Teach **8** defensive role of the puck-side wing. An offensive player (X3) is in the corner with the puck. X3 attempts to pass to the puck-side defenseman (X1). The puck-side wing (LW) checks X1 closely, preventing him from either receiving the puck or moving to the puck.

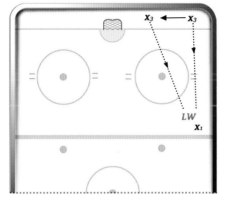

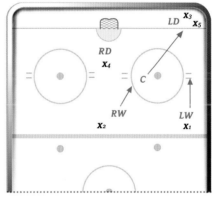

Purpose: Teach the **9** wings proper position while covering the points. The puck-side wing (LW) must cover his point man (X1) closely. He does this by staying within a stick's length and playing a little to X1's left. This prevents X1 from moving past the LW. The off-side wing (RW) plays his point (X2) more loosely (10 to 12 feet away). The RW plays to X2's right. This prevents quick access to the high slot for X2. Both wings must watch the puck and their respective points.

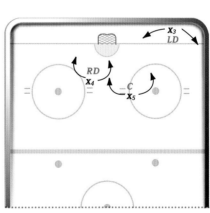

Purpose: Teach defensive **10** the interaction of the center and the two defensemen. An offensive player (X3) has the puck in the corner. One defenseman (LD) covers X3. The RD and the center set up according to the position of X4 and X5. Drill is essentially a 3-on-3. Defensive players must control their checks and gain possession of the puck.

Purpose: Teach defensive **11** role of the off-side wing. An offensive player (X3) is in the corner with the puck. X3 attempts to pass to the off-side defenseman (X2). The off-side wing (RW), positioned between the puck and X2, attempts to intercept the puck. If the puck reaches the point, the RW prevents X2 from shooting or moving to the net.

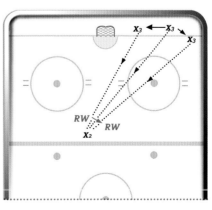

OFFENSIVE PLAY

ON DEFENSE, YOU ATTACK THE PUCK. ON OFFENSE, YOU ATTACK *WITH* THE puck. Offensive play is a blitzkrieg, an all-out attempt to overwhelm the other team with speed and strength and dazzling creativity. Much more room for innovation exists when your team goes on the offensive; in fact, quick reaction, unexpected adjustments and novelty are the essence of good offense. A goal scored is the ultimate unanticipated play, and the best systems of offense are the frameworks that generate the most opportunities for players to come up with something that no one is expecting.

Passing is crucial to success. Offense is all about moving the puck, and while there are times when one player carries the puck, for the most part, the puck should be advanced by passing. There isn't a player alive who can move at the speed of a brisk pass, and if a team is going to reap the rewards of effective offensive systems, then they must possess good passing skills. That means eliminating selfish play.

The players' individual strengths and weaknesses will be the main determinant of which offensive system the coach should choose. Fast-skating teams benefit from different systems than teams that emphasize size and strength. The former will likely use systems geared to open ice, while the latter are more apt to use those that direct play along the boards.

Readers will notice that this section of the book appears much more detailed than the material on defensive systems. That is because while defense is all about positioning and responding, offense is about decisive action—one thing leads to the next thing, which leads to the next. Despite the detail, coaches should keep in mind that these systems are, if anything, oversimplifications. As anyone who watches hockey knows, every moment contains infinite possibilities.

Coaches should also note that there is less and less direction possible (or desirable) as the offense moves into the opponents' end of the rink. Care and method are required to move the puck safely out of your own end, but from that point on, the possibilities for creativity and novelty should steadily increase.

*The players are out not only to make a good pass
but to try to find a situation in which this pass will
be most convenient and useful for their partners.
And having made the pass, they once again strive
to find themselves an opening to be on the
receiving end this time.*

Anatoli Tarasov
The Road to Olympus

BREAKOUTS

BREAKOUT, OFFENSIVE PLAY IN YOUR OWN END, IS PERHAPS THE MOST crucial systematic element of the offense. The attack begins when the offensive team regains possession of the puck. Successful breakout plays do two things: First, they allow the offense to clear its own zone; and second, they force the opposition to play defense.

The systems for breakout plays are not complicated. They are deliberately kept simple, because in your own end, it is execution that counts. Each player must know what everyone else's responsibility is as well as his own. Breakout plays succeed when everyone is in sync with everyone else. Breakouts call for teamwork.

Breakout plays should be worked on in every practice. Drills that utilize the entire ice surface—for example, a 5-on-2 line rush—should be started as breakouts, and the coach determines the success of the breakout plays by instilling the essential discipline into the team.

Although there are not a lot of different systems for breakout plays, plenty of options exist within that limited number. Teams should go slowly when learning breakouts. As they progress, the options increase.

Coaches should keep in mind that breakouts especially benefit from moving the puck quickly and that the best way to do that is to pass the puck. It is the ability of the team to utilize the passing options that strengthens its attack. A sound attack begins with sound breakout plays, because the entire attack is dependent on the offensive team leaving its own end with confidence.

POSITIONAL PLAY

Virtually the first thing that young hockey players learn from coaches is where their positions are on the ice. The left wing is on the left, the right wing on the right, etc. Positional play at any level of experience is premised on the wings, the center and the defensemen all staying in the lanes and the areas for which they are responsible. The Positional Play breakout is a conservative system. A forward is always in position to assume a defensive role if the puck is turned over. It is a balanced approach that utilizes all the players, and the offensive team can break out along either wing or up the middle. All teams must be familiar with this system; situations arise in every game that require it. The Positional Play breakout is especially important for young teams and for those with limited skating ability.

KEY POINTS

1. The Positional Play system is a conservative one with basic principles.

2. It stresses that one forward always be in position to move immediately to the defense if the puck is turned over.

3. It emphasizes high-percentage passes.

4. The defensemen "quarterback" the play.

5. It is a balanced system designed to use all three forwards, although it can be altered to emphasize a specific position.

6. Wings may cut across the middle to receive passes, but for the most part, everyone plays his lane.

DEFENSEMAN TO WING (A)

A defenseman swings behind the net with the puck and passes to a wing on the boards. The wing has a number of options.

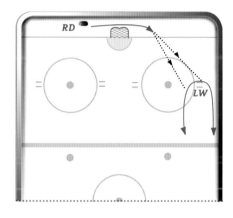

1 The defenseman (RD) has the puck and carries it behind the net. Without stopping, he passes to the LW. The LW can carry it up the ice.

The LW passes **2** to the center, who is moving toward him. The RW has a number of options: staying behind and following as a third forward, moving up his wing or moving across the ice.

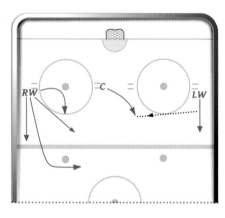

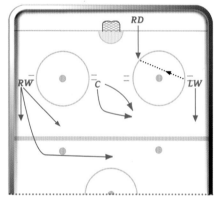

3 The LW passes back to the RD, who has continued up the ice after his initial pass. The RD can carry the puck or pass to any of the three forwards.

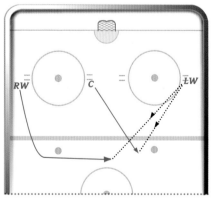

4 The LW can pass to the center or to the RW in the neutral zone.

DEFENSEMAN TO WING (B)

A defenseman carries the puck behind the net and passes to a wing cutting across the face-off circle. The wing has a number of options.

The defenseman **1** (RD) has the puck and carries it behind the net. Stopping behind the net, he passes to the LW, who cuts across the face-off circle. The LW can carry the puck.

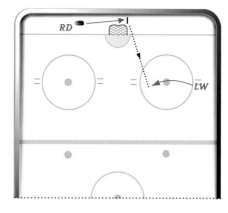

The LW **2** passes to the center, who can move in a number of directions.

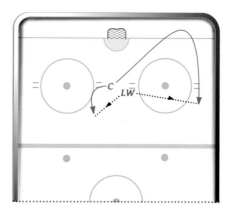

The LW **3** passes to the RW, who is either on his own wing or has moved to the middle.

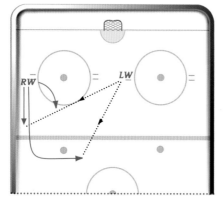

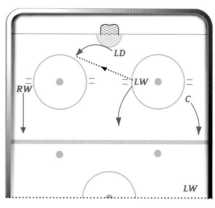

4 The LW passes to the LD, who can carry the puck or redirect it to any of the three forwards.

DEFENSEMAN TO WING (C)

A defenseman carries the puck behind the net and passes to a wing angling across inside the blue line. The wing has a number of options.

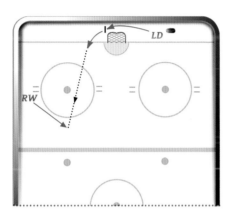

1 The defenseman (LD) has the puck and carries it behind the net. Stopping behind the net, the LD passes to the RW, who is angling across the zone toward the blue line.

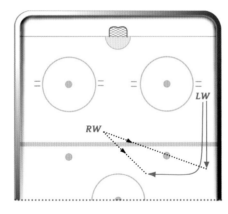

2 The RW passes to the LW, who is either moving toward the neutral zone or has already moved to that zone and is cutting across it toward the middle of the ice.

The RW passes to the center, who has moved in behind the RW's normal position. **3**

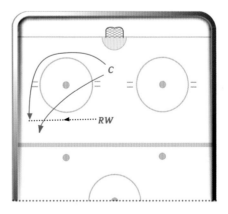

DEFENSEMAN TO CENTER (A)

A defenseman has the puck behind the net and passes to the center, who has moved into the corner. The center has a number of options.

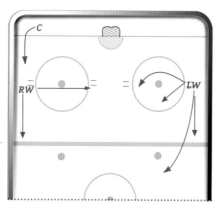

1 The defenseman (LD) has the puck and carries it behind the net. The center swings into a corner. The LD passes to the center.

When the center **2** swings into the corner, the wings have a number of options.

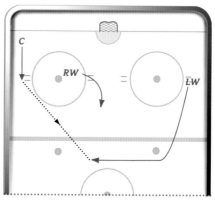

3 One example has the center passing to the LW, who has moved to the neutral zone and is cutting across it. The RW moves up the middle.

When the center moves up the ice with **4** the puck, the opposition has a tendency to move as a unit with him. This permits a defenseman (RD) to move up the ice behind the play. The RD is usually open, and the center passes back to him. The RD has a number of options.

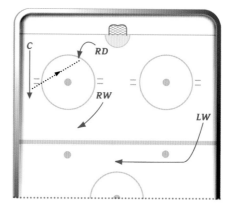

DEFENSEMAN TO CENTER (B)

A defenseman swings behind the net with the puck and passes to the center in the slot. The center has a number of options.

The defenseman (RD) has **1** the puck and carries it behind the net. Without stopping, he passes to the center, who is skating across the slot. The center can carry it up the ice.

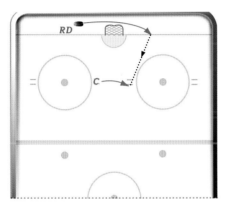

2 The center passes to the LW, who is skating on his wing.

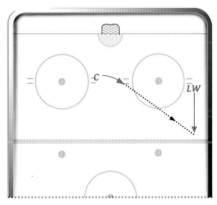

3 The center passes to the RW, who is skating on his wing or coming across the ice either at an angle or by swinging out past the blue line.

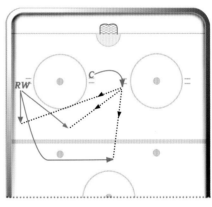

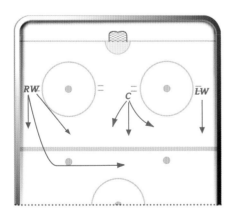

4 The forwards, working as a unit, each have specific avenues available.

DEFENSEMAN TO DEFENSEMAN

A defenseman has the puck behind the net and passes to the other defenseman, who has moved into the corner.

The defenseman (RD) has the puck and carries it behind the net. Stopping behind the net, the RD passes to the LD, who has swung into the corner.

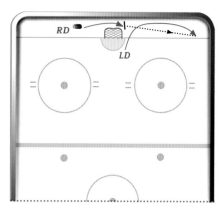

The LD passes to the center, who has a number of options.

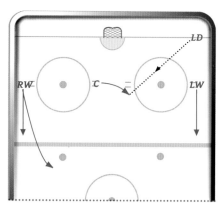

The LD passes to the RW, who has moved to the slot area after the LD vacated it.

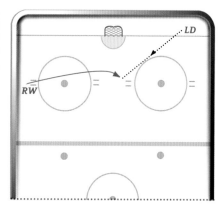

When the LD moves up along the boards, the RD often is open as the opposition also moves up the ice. The RD is able to move up the open slot area. The LD passes back to the RD.

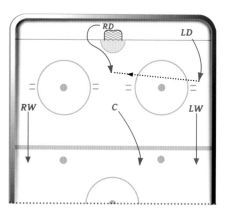

CENTER AND DEFENSEMAN SWING INTO CORNER

A defenseman has the puck behind the net and passes to the center or to the other defenseman in the corner.

The defenseman (RD) has the puck behind the net and has stopped. The center and the LD swing into opposite corners.

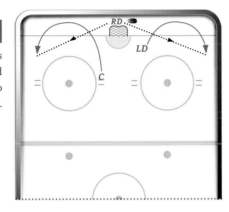

When the center and the LD swing into the corners, the RW and the LW have a number of directions they can move.

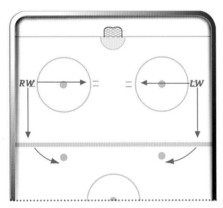

One possible play has the LD passing to the RW, who has cut across the slot. The RW has a number of options.

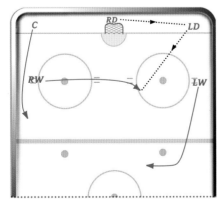

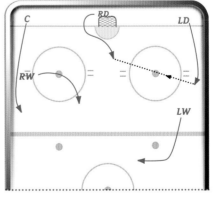

When the LD moves up the ice with the puck, the opposition has a tendency to move up the ice as a unit. The RD can move up the slot and is open for a pass back from the LD. The RD has a number of options.

73

BOARD PLAY

This is a conservative system with a limited number of options. The breakout passes are along the boards to the wings. No team should use this technique as its only system for breaking out, though it may be used as the predominant method of clearing the zone. This system best suits teams with big, strong wings who can dominate their check and count on winning the battle for the puck along the boards. It is important for the team to have forwards willing to be physical in these areas of combat. Small forwards, to play this system, must be adept at picking the puck up off the boards while moving. The wings are the *key* players in this system.

KEY POINTS

1. Board Play is a conservative style with objectives that are simple and direct.

2. The puck is directed toward the boards and away from the middle and the slot.

3. It is a balanced system, with both boards used equally.

4. The objective is to control the boards. This means controlling the puck and the opposition.

5. The wings are the key players in this system.

6. This style is called Board Play because the boards are used for *passing*.

7. Board Play is useful to defensemen who are under pressure.

BOARD PASS
*Defenseman passes to
wing using the boards.*

The defenseman **1** (RD) has the puck and passes to the LW using the boards.

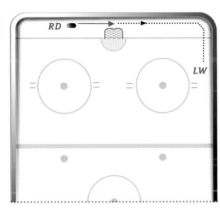

2 The LW passes to the center.

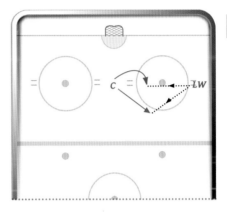

The LW passes **3** to the RW.

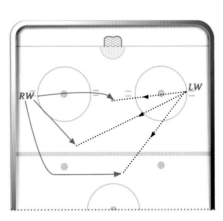

The LW passes **4** back to the LD, who can carry the puck or pass again to one of the three forwards.

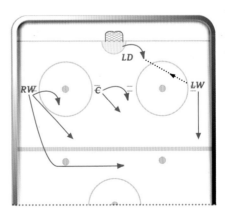

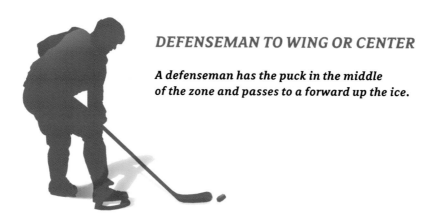

DEFENSEMAN TO WING OR CENTER

A defenseman has the puck in the middle of the zone and passes to a forward up the ice.

1 A defenseman (LD) has the puck in the middle of the defensive zone. The LD passes to the LW.

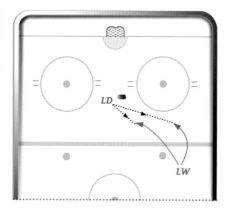

2 Two forwards (C and RW) crisscross near the blue line. The LD can pass to either.

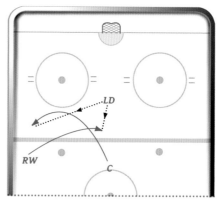

3 The initial pass to a forward should be followed with a quick second pass to another forward. For example, the LD passes to the LW, who quickly moves the puck to the RW.

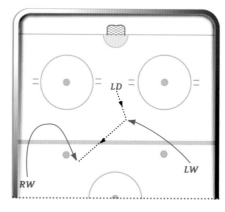

FLOOD THE ZONE

A defenseman has the puck deep behind the goal line. The other defenseman and two forwards flood the zone, creating three possible pass routes.

A defenseman (RD) has the puck deep behind the goal line. Three players (RW, C and LD) move in front of the RD. The LW normally moves to the net to cover for the LD.

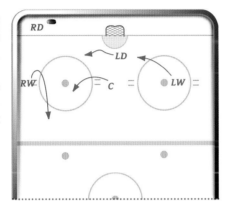

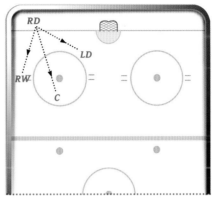

2 The RD can pass to any of the three players: the RW, the LD or the center.

3 For example, the RD passes to the center.

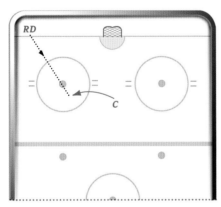

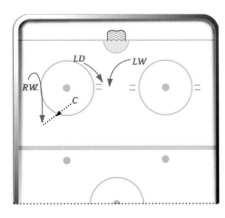

4 The center moves the puck quickly to the RW, who is skating in the zone.

FREE-FLOWING (A)

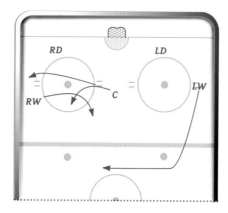

1 **Basic Pattern.**
The LW moves to the neutral zone and skates across it. The RW and the center swing back through the face-off circle and may or may not crisscross. The defensemen (LD and RD) have the option of passing to any open forward.

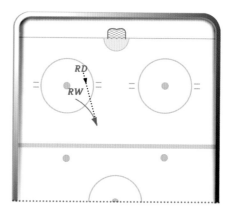

2 For example, the RD passes to the RW.

The RW **3** passes to either the center or the LW.

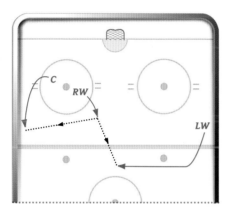

4 Whichever forward receives the pass from the defenseman has the option of passing to either of the other two forwards, who are skating into an open area.

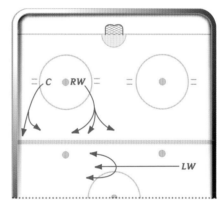

FREE-FLOWING (B)

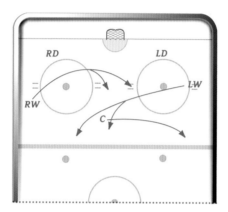

1 **Basic Pattern.** The center swings to one side and can move to the neutral zone. The RW cuts deep across the zone and moves up the middle. The LW cuts across the middle of the zone toward the other side. The defensemen (LD and RD) have the option of passing to any open forward.

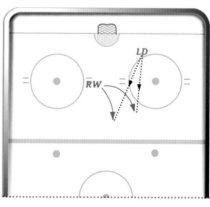

2 For example, the LD passes to the RW.

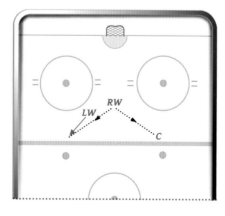

3 The RW passes to either the center or the LW.

FREE-FLOWING (C)

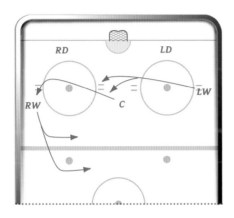

1 **Basic Pattern.**
The RW moves toward the blue line, cutting across on either side of it. The LW swings deep and up the middle. The center swings into the normal position of the RW. The defensemen (LD and RD) have the option of passing to any open forward.

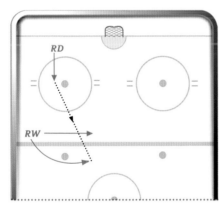

2 For example, the RD passes to the RW.

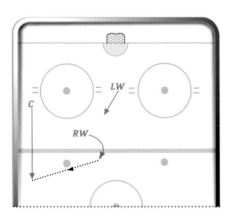

3 The RW passes to the center. The LW follows up the play.

DRILLS

A good method of teaching breakout plays through drills is to do the following:

• Demonstrate the proper positioning and the various options of the play;

• Have the players walk through the play (half speed);

• Have the team execute the play (three-quarters progressing to full speed);

• Increase the difficulty of the play by inserting the opposition's players.

• Many of the steps can be made into drills for 1-on-1s, 2-on-1s, 3-on-2s, etc.

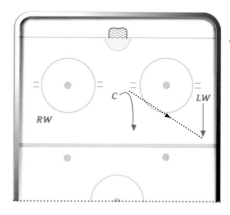

1A The center can pass to the LW or carry the puck.

Defenseman to Forward Demonstration and Walkthrough

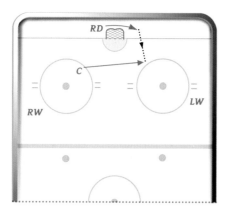

1 The defenseman (RD) swings behind the net and passes to the center, who is coming across the slot.

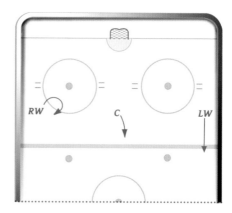

1B The three forwards break out of the zone, with the RW coming from behind. (This can develop into a 3-on-1 or a 3-on-2 drill.)

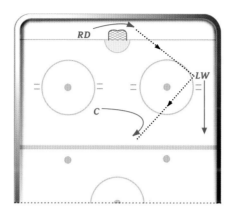

2 The RD swings behind the net and passes to the LW, who is either stationary on the boards or moving up the ice. The LW carries the puck up the ice. (This can develop into a 1-on-1 drill.) Or the LW can pass to the center, who is moving up the middle. (This can develop into a 2-on-1 drill.)

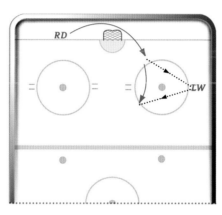

3 The RD swings behind the net and passes to the LW. The RD continues to move up the ice and receives a return pass (give and go) from the LW. (This can develop into a 1-on-1 or a 2-on-1 drill.)

4 The RW is inserted into Steps 4 and 5. The off-side wing (RW) moves a couple of strides toward the slot. This prevents him from getting ahead of the play and teaches him his defensive role. (This can develop into a 3-on-1 or a 3-on-2 drill.)

5 **Walkthrough and Execution**
Practice the above options 5-on-0. Be sure to cover each option.

6 **Execution With Difficulty**
Insert one forechecker (X5) to forecheck the puck. The LD should screen out X5 as part of the drill.

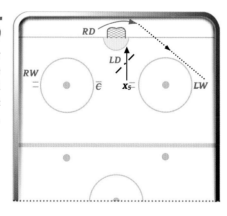

7 Insert more forecheckers. It is this step that begins to simulate gamelike conditions.

8 The forechecking unit works systematically. The offensive unit needs to be able to clear the zone against a full forechecking unit in practice to gain the confidence to do so in a game.

9 Have short scrimmages (10 to 15 seconds) by starting at different points in the breakout play.

DRILLS

Board Play Demonstration and Walkthrough

1 The defenseman (RD) passes the puck along the boards to the near wing (RW).

The RW carries the **2A** puck out of the zone. (This can develop into a 1-on-1 drill.)

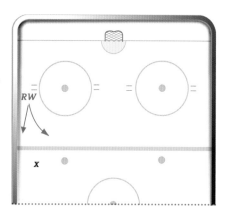

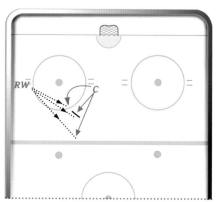

2B The RW passes to the center, who is swinging toward the boards, moving up the ice or setting a pick (to work a give and go with the RW). (This can develop into a 2-on-1 drill.)

The three forwards move out of the **3** defensive zone as a unit. The LW moves toward the slot area (for defensive purposes) and comes from behind the play. (This can develop into a 3-on-1 or a 3-on-2 drill.)

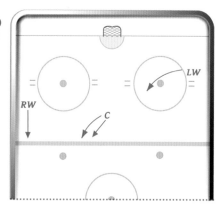

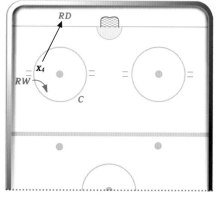

4 Insert one forechecker (X4), who forechecks the puck and the RD. Either the RW or the center should interfere with X4 to give the RD more time.

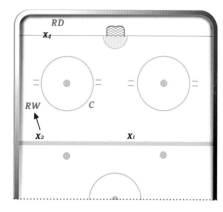

5 Insert a second forechecker (X2), who pinches along the boards on the RW. The RW must control the boards. If the RW is not able to control the puck, he must immediately check X2. (This can develop into a 1-on-1 or a 2-on-1 drill, with the opposition's other defenseman, X1, being the defenseman.)

6 Insert the other members of the forechecking unit. It is this step that begins to simulate gamelike conditions. The forechecking unit works systematically. The offensive unit needs to be able to clear the zone against a full forechecking unit in practice to gain the confidence to do so in a game.

7 Have short scrimmages (10 to 15 seconds) by starting at different points in the breakout play.

***Free-Flowing Play
Demonstration
and Walkthrough***

The defenseman (RD)
passes the puck to the
RW. The RW practices the
different routes available
to him. (This can develop
into a 1-on-1 drill.) **1**

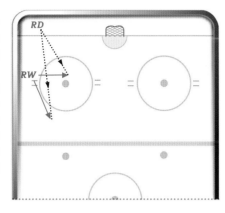

2 The defenseman
(RD) passes the puck
to the center. The center
practices the different
routes available to him.
(This can develop into a
1-on-1 drill.)

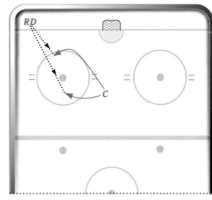

The defenseman (RD)
passes the puck to the
LW. The LW practices the
different routes available
to him. (This can develop
into a 1-on-1 drill.) **3**

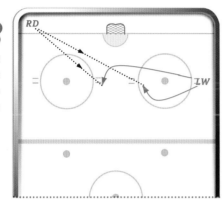

4 The defenseman
(RD) passes the
puck to either the center
or the RW. The LW simul-
taneously moves to the
neutral zone. (This can
develop into a 2-on-1, a
3-on-1 or a 3-on-2 drill.)

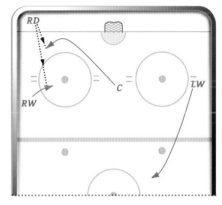

The three forwards
break out of the
defensive zone, with the
RD making the outlet pass.
(This can develop into a
3-on-1 or a 3-on-2 drill.) **5**

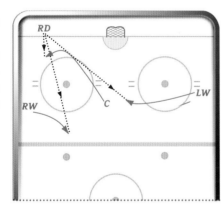

6 The coach goes through
the different patterns.
The forwards, in particular,
must be familiar with each
option. The defensive responsibilities must be clearly
understood.

Insert one
forechecker (X3)
to forecheck the puck.
The above steps can be
executed with the
one forechecker. **7**

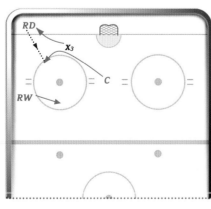

8 Insert more forecheckers. It is this
step that begins to simulate gamelike
conditions.

10 Have short scrimmages (10 to 15
seconds) by starting at different
points in the breakout plays.

9 The forechecking
unit works system-
atically. The offensive unit
needs to be able to clear
the zone against a full
forechecking unit in practice to gain the confidence
to do so in a game.

Although not every coach can win consistently with talent, no coach can win without it.

John Wooden
They Call Me Coach

NEUTRAL ZONE OFFENSE

H ISTORICALLY, COACHES HAVE OFTEN OVERLOOKED NEUTRAL ZONE offensive play. It was as if the offense just passed through the center-ice no-man's-land on its way to the scoring zone at the other end of the rink. In reality, effective neutral zone play translates into a better attack, and most often, the team that wins the battle in the neutral zone wins the game. An offensive squad that can make its way decisively across the neutral zone crosses the opponents' blue line with initiative and tempo on its side; the defenders, on the other hand, are set back on their heels, scrambling to reorganize.

The objective of neutral zone offense is to generate the attack. The better the execution, the quicker and stronger the attack. Offensive play in this zone is either the counterattack, which follows regaining possession of the puck in the center-ice area, or the attack link between the breakout and the offensive melée in the opponents' end.

The systems of attack that a team employs should therefore be consistent from zone to zone, and the offensive play and individual responsibilities must be similar for the players whether the play is a counterattack or the attack link. It is crucial that the players have a thorough understanding of the principles of their system and that they be taught to use their time in the neutral zone effectively and not just skate for the other end of the rink.

As always, the coach must keep in mind his personnel's abilities when selecting a system for the neutral zone, and he should give careful consideration to this under-appreciated aspect of the game when he is making plans and deciding on offensive strategies.

This chapter has two parts. Part One presents three basic systems of neutral zone play: Positional Play, Forwards Crisscross and Regroup/Free Movement. This section suggests systems that provide the guiding principles to neutral zone offense. Part Two presents a number of specific plays and suggests ways to generate the attack as it moves over the blue line into the offensive zone.

POSITIONAL PLAY

The Positional Play system in the neutral zone is a conservative one that complements the Positional Play breakout system. It is a balanced system that utilizes all the players. The basic traditional positions have the wings in the outside lanes, the defensemen in the inner lanes and the center in the middle. A forward is always in position to assume a defensive role if the puck is turned over. This system calls for short, direct, high-percentage passes. All teams, regardless of their ability, must be familiar with this system because situations requiring it arise during every game that every team plays. It also is a foundation for all systems of play in the neutral zone. This system is especially beneficial for teams with size and/or poor skating ability.

KEY POINTS

1. The Positional Play system is a conservative style of offense. It is easy to teach, since everyone simply plays his position.

2. It stresses playing and controlling the neutral zone's lanes.

3. It emphasizes a basic style of play: head-man passes, short and direct passes, 2-on-1 situations, etc.

4. This system emphasizes control of the boards in the neutral zone.

5. "Dumping the puck" is permitted but only as a predetermined play. One forward must be in position to get to the puck first or quick enough to pressure the opposition if possession of the puck is lost.

6. The defensemen are conservative. They primarily move the puck to the forwards. When they move up, they do so to fill a lane.

7. Positional Play enforces the discipline needed to win the neutral zone.

This system allows some interchanging of the lanes. The wings and the defensemen are allowed to move between two lanes, while the center is allowed to play all five.

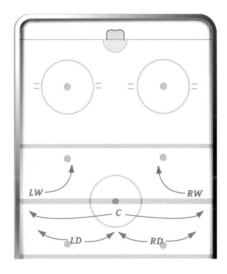

The normal procedure has the wings staying in their lanes. If a wing (LW) moves to another lane, three things can happen:

1) The center moves to the wing's lane;
2) A defenseman (LD) moves to the wing's lane;
3) The LW and the center create a 2-on-1 situation as they double up on one of the two opposing defensemen.

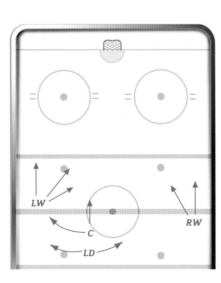

If a wing (LW) is ahead of the play, the center has to headman the puck to the LW, who either stays in his lane or moves over a lane. The center reacts to the LW's play. The LD can move up to fill a lane or remain at his position.

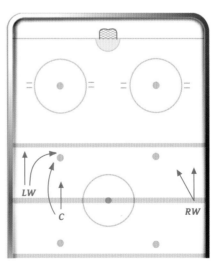

If the LW is skating but covered, the center can clear the red line and dump the puck if he thinks the LW can get to it first. The LW can also cut across the blue line and set a pick to clear a lane for the center.

If the wings are coming from behind the play, the center has a number of options:

He holds the **4A** puck and sets up a 2-on-1 situation against a defenseman (X1). The wings must break; i.e., head straight for the blue line.

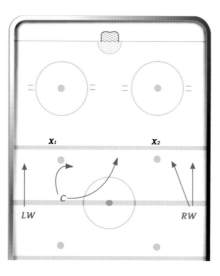

He swings wide and carries the **4B** puck deep along the boards with the wing (LW) following. This creates a 2-on-1 situation on a defenseman (X1) in a vertical alignment.

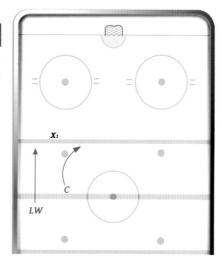

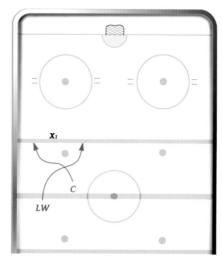

4C He cuts to the boards, and the wing (LW) cuts to the middle. This creates a different 2-on-1 situation on a defenseman (X1).

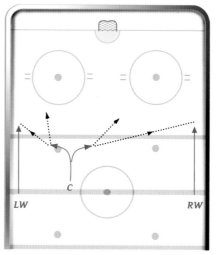

4D He slows down or stops close to the blue line, permitting the wings to break in for a pass or to be in position to gain possession of the puck if it is dumped in.

If the defensemen have the **5A** puck, they should never keep it and force the forwards to stop skating. Their responsibility is to move the puck and keep the forwards skating. The forwards can move up the ice or across into other lanes.

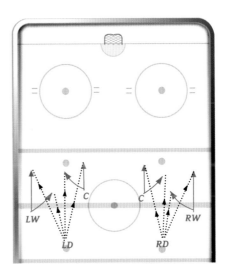

The defensemen can work a give **5B** and go. The defenseman (LD) passes to a wing (LW) and moves up to receive a return pass, creating a 2-on-1 situation on the defenseman (X1) for the LD and the center.

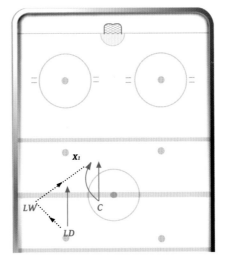

If the forwards are covered but **5C** skating, the defenseman (LD) can dump the puck and two forwards (LW and C) will converge on it.

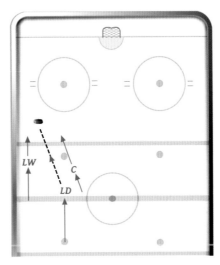

FORWARDS CRISSCROSS

The Forwards Crisscross system combines conservatism with free movement. The conservative aspect of this system is that one forward, usually a wing, remains in a stable position with defensive responsibilities if the puck is turned over. The extra freedom is a result of the two remaining forwards being encouraged to move laterally and to flood specific areas. For example, the RW stays in his lane while the center and the LW crisscross. This system can be used by any team once it has mastered the Positional Play system. The players must have competent skating and puck-handling skills if this system is to be effective.

KEY POINTS

1. The Forwards Crisscross system combines conservatism with limited free movement. The "limits" make it easy to teach.

2. It emphasizes quick skating and crisp passing.

3. One forward has a static or nonmoving role. He becomes the safety valve for the defensemen and often relays the puck to the two skating forwards.

4. Dumping the puck should be used only as a last resort. If it is done, the puck should be directed to an area on which the skating forwards can quickly converge.

5. The defensemen are conservative. They usually move the puck to the forwards. When they move up, it is done to fill a lane.

The off-side wing (RW) goes to the boards. The puck-side wing (LW) and the center crisscross. The crisscrossing can be done in any number of patterns (Diagrams 1a-1b). The LD will normally move the puck to the skating forwards. He may pass to the RD, who then passes to the skating forwards. The different patterns allow the forwards to find open spaces.

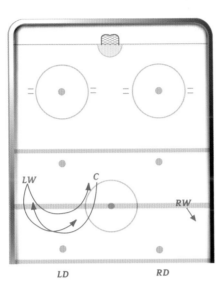

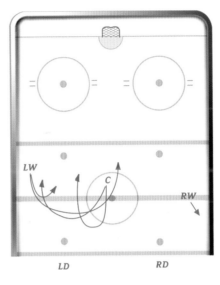

The off-side wing (RW) plays a key role. He provides stability because he is always on the boards. He is the safety valve and is often in position to relay the puck from the defensemen to the skating forwards.

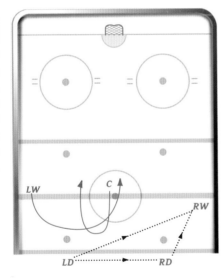

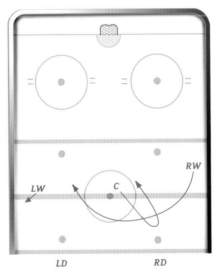

A variation of this neutral zone offense is to have the puck-side wing (LW) go to the boards while the off-side wing (RW) and the center crisscross.

This variation can be used when the opposition has a particular weak side. The crisscrossing forwards should move toward the LD for a quick pass.

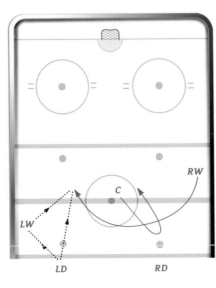

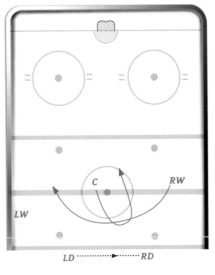

If the LD makes a quick pass to the RD, then the LW becomes the off-side wing and the system reverts to the mirror image of that shown in Diagrams 1 and 2.

REGROUP/FREE MOVEMENT

The Regroup/Free Movement system abandons the traditional conservative aspects of neutral zone play. The forwards are always skating, looking for or creating openings. Puck control is essential for this system. Players regroup in order to control the puck until an opening to the offensive zone is found, then the forwards attack that opening. The free-movement aspect permits the forwards maneuverability in the zone. It is an aggressive system in the sense that the forwards remain in constant motion, ready for quick movement toward any area. It is important for the coach to emphasize that the freewheeling forwards still have defensive responsibilities in the event of a turnover. This system can be employed only by teams with a high level of skill development.

KEY POINTS

1. The Regroup/Free Movement system calls for constant motion from the forwards.

2. The constant motion makes it a difficult system to teach in a short period of time.

3. Skillful puck handling is vital.

4. The objective is to control the puck until the forwards are able to create an opening into the offensive zone.

5. The defensemen quarterback the play but are also permitted to move into the openings.

6. Advanced development of the technical skills—skating, passing and stickhandling—is crucial for this system to be successful.

Diagrams 1A-1D illustrate four of the more intricate patterns available to teams with greater skating ability. (These can be skating drills.)

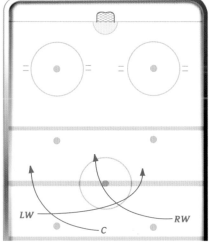

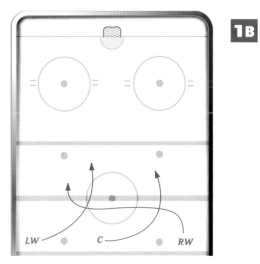

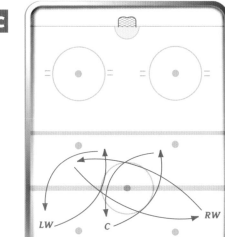

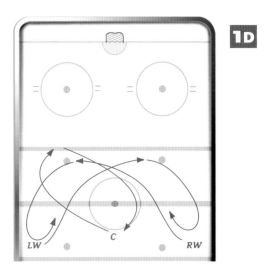

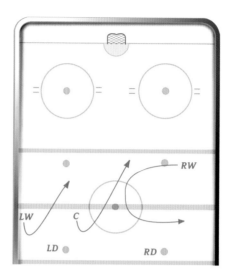

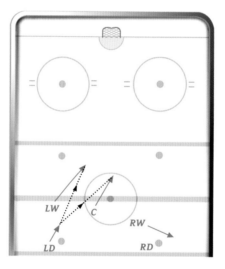

2A The coach must limit the number of patterns with specific guidelines. For example, if the forward farthest from the puck (RW) has the defensive role, the other two forwards have unlimited freedom to create an opening. The RW can become a decoy. For example, the RW can cut across the red line and turn back toward the defensemen. The RW stays in position defensively. If the RW has been successful in clearing the

2B defensive forward from the area, the center and the LW will move to the area, and the defenseman with the puck (LD) will know that that is the potential opening and be prepared to move the puck in that direction.

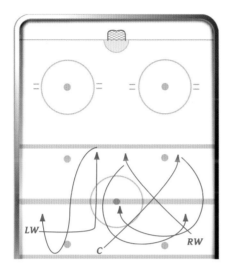

3A If an opening is not created on the initial rush, the forwards regroup, move back toward the defensemen and make another rush. Skating ability and puck control make this tactic possible. Often the forwards turn back with the puck and pass back to the defensemen to initiate the regrouping.

Regrouping can be a tactical move. **3B** The opposition may have a tendency to break down or get out of position during regrouping. The forwards will look for a player who gets out of position and attack that area. For example, the opposition's left defenseman (X2) may move up the ice too quickly when the offensive unit regroups.

The RW and the center will regroup, while the LW will move toward the area X2 may vacate. The two defensemen will anticipate this. The LD passes to the RD, who will pass to the LW if he is open.

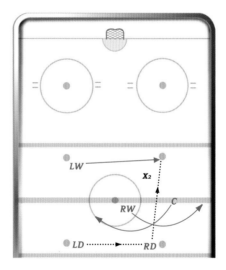

NEUTRAL ZONE ATTACK

This section presents plays for entering the offensive zone. These are not systems but more specific suggestions for the patterns of players as they move into the opponents' end of the rink. Players need to know this kind of information so that they will discipline their play as they attack across the far blue line. These plays are good practice drills. The coach should teach several of these plays, but not all of them. Hockey is not like basketball, where the coach is able to call out the plays as the team moves up the court. Include these plays in 2-on-1 and 3-on-2 drills. Whether the drill starts at the red line, the far blue line or the far end, the players need to have an idea of what is going to happen as they move up the ice. Practicing plays that emphasize entering the offensive zone accomplishes this.

KEY POINTS

1. Players must have a general idea of what they are going to do while moving up the ice.

2. The team should be familiar with a limited number of plays, not a large number.

3. The plays must permit a flexible framework that encourages innovation.

4. Entering the offensive zone as a coordinated unit intensifies the attack.

DUMP THE PUCK

A wing has the puck and shoots it deep to the opposite corner. The other wing is skating toward the corner to regain control of the puck.

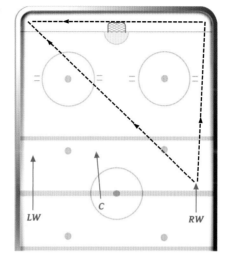

1 The RW has control of the puck, clears the red line and shoots it deep into the LW's corner. This is done either diagonally or around the boards. The LW is skating toward the corner.

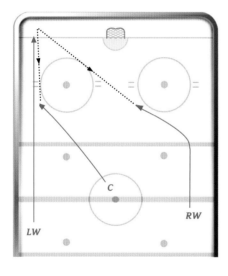

2 The LW has the puck deep in the corner. The center moves to the left side and is in a position to follow or back up the LW. The RW moves to the slot. The LW has the option of passing to either forward.

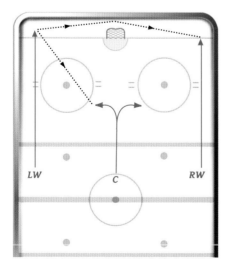

3 The LW has the puck deep in the corner. The RW goes deep on his wing. The center moves to the slot. The LW has the option of passing to either forward.

CENTER CONTROLS THE PUCK (A)

The center has control of the puck and passes to a wing.

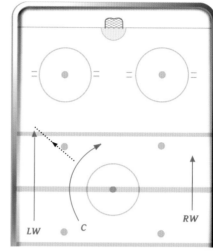

1 The center has control of the puck and cuts first toward the left wing and then back toward the middle. The center passes to the LW.

2 The center makes this move in an effort to get the opposition's defenseman (X1) to move with him toward the middle. If X1 moves toward the middle, the outside lane opens for the LW.

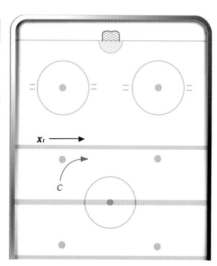

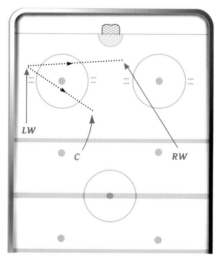

3 The LW has the puck entering the offensive zone. The center moves to the slot. The RW goes directly to the net (the goal post on his side). The LW has the option of passing to either forward.

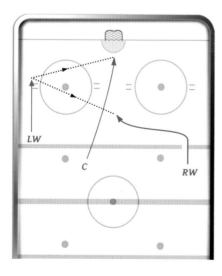

4 The LW has the puck entering the offensive zone. The center moves to the net. The RW moves across to the slot. The LW has the option of passing to either forward.

The center has control of the puck. He moves to the left side and ahead of the LW. The center crosses the blue line, carries the puck along the boards and either back passes or makes a drop pass to the LW.

1

CENTER CONTROLS THE PUCK (B)

The center has the puck and carries it across the blue line.

The center carries the puck along the boards. This is done to make the opposition's defenseman (X1) turn and move with him. This opens up the LW for the pass.

2

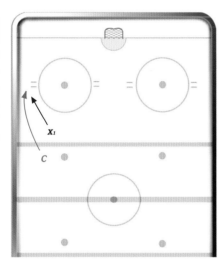

3 The LW has the puck near the blue line. The center continues deep along the boards. The RW goes directly to the net (the goal post on his side). The LW has the option of passing to either forward.

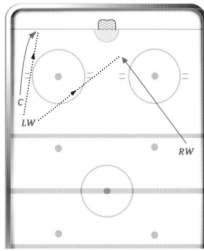

4 The LW has the puck near the blue line. The center moves to the net area. The RW moves across to the slot. The LW has the option of passing to either forward.

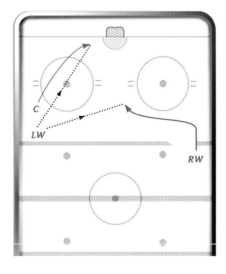

CENTER CONTROLS THE PUCK (C)

The center has control of the puck and carries it into the offensive zone.

1 The center carries the puck into the offensive zone and stops inside the blue line.

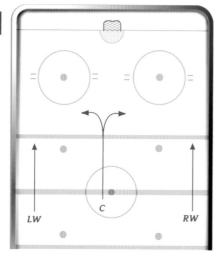

2 The center passes quickly to the wing (LW) while the other wing (RW) moves to the net area. The LW passes to the RW.

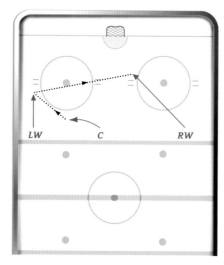

3 Both wings (LW and RW) move deep toward the net. The center has the option of passing to either wing.

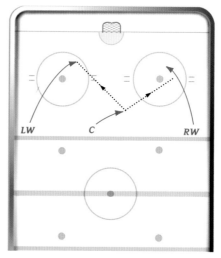

WING CONTROLS THE PUCK

A wing has control of the puck and cuts toward the middle, near the blue line.

1 The LW has control of the puck and cuts to the middle, near the blue line. The center cuts to the left side, behind the LW. The RW stays along the boards. The LW can make a drop pass to the center.

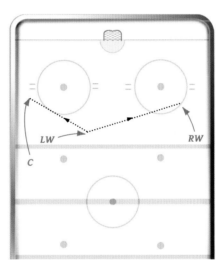

2 The LW has the puck near the blue line. The RW and the center move along the boards. The LW has the option of passing to either forward.

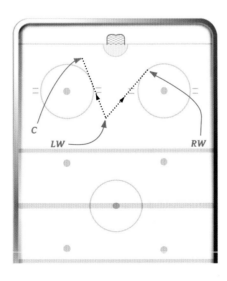

3 The LW carries the puck into the slot area. The center and the RW move deep into the slot area. The LW has the option of passing to either forward.

The center has control of the puck and moves to the left side. Both wings stay on their wings. The LD moves into the area vacated by the center.

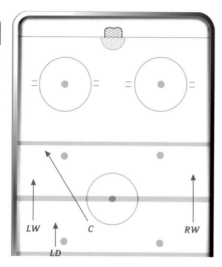

DEFENSEMAN MOVES UP THE PLAY

A defenseman moves up on the play in the neutral zone, filling a lane.

The LW stays back, while the LD moves into the offensive play.

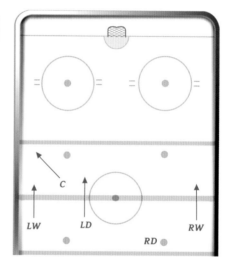

The center carries the puck into the offensive zone. The RW cuts across into the high slot. The LD moves through the slot to the net area. The center has the option of passing to either the LD or the RW.

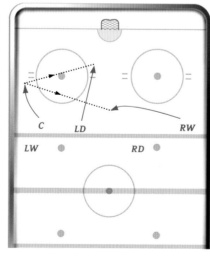

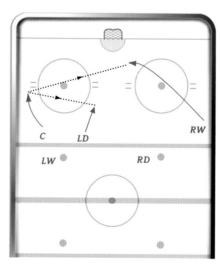

The center carries the puck into the offensive zone. The RW moves to the net area. The LD goes to the high slot. The center has the option of passing to either the RW or the LD.

The skating patterns of the three forwards while they are regrouping in the neutral zone.

1

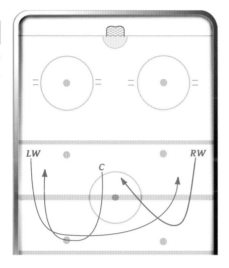

FORWARDS REGROUP

The three forwards regroup in the neutral zone. This is done after the initial attempt to move into the offensive zone is stopped.

The center **2** has the puck and passes back to the RD. The three forwards skate their patterns.

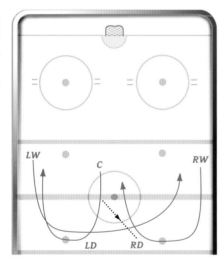

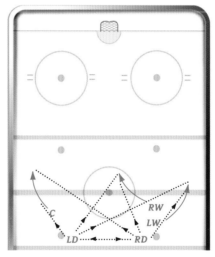

There are a **3** number of possible passing plays. The RD and the LD can pass to the forwards any time during their regrouping patterns.

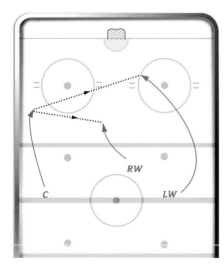

The center has **4** received the puck and carries it into the offensive zone. The LW moves along the right board deep into the zone. The RW moves up the middle toward the high slot. The center has the option of passing to either the LW or the RW.

QUICK TRANSITION (A)

A defenseman gains control of the puck in the neutral zone, and the forwards quickly move to the offensive.

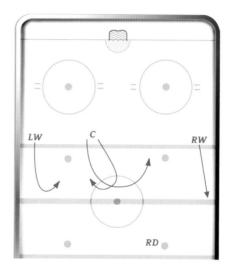

1 The first forward back to the neutral zone (RW) goes to the boards. The center and the LW swing within their normal lanes.

2 The LD has control of the puck. He can pass to any of the forwards to start the transition.

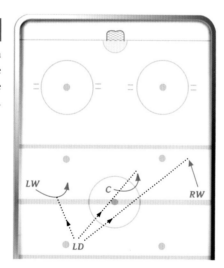

3 The LD passes to the RD, who can pass to any of the forwards to start the transition.

The transition attempts to trap the opposition's forwards (X3, X4 and X5) and to create a 3-on-2 attack. **4**

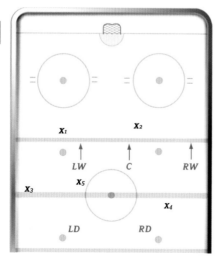

QUICK TRANSITION (B)

A defenseman gains control of the puck in the neutral zone, and the forwards quickly move to the offensive.

The center goes directly to the boards at the red line. The other two forwards (LW and RW) crisscross.

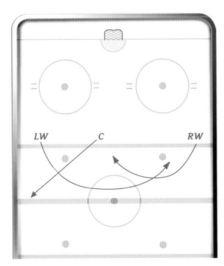

2 The LD has control of the puck. He can pass to any of the forwards to start the transition.

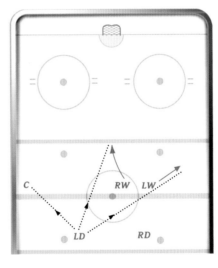

The LD passes to the RD, who can pass to any of the forwards to start the transition.

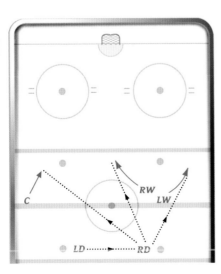

4 The transition attempts to trap the opposition's forwards (X3, X4 and X5) and to create a 3-on-2 attack.

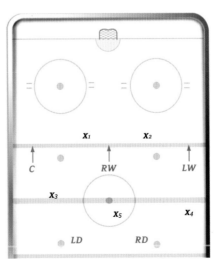

No matter how exciting a game may be
from the point of view of tactics or technique,
it will not be interesting if the tactics
do not result in a goal being scored.

Anatoli Tarasov
The Road to Olympus

OFFENSIVE ZONE PLAY

THE OBJECTIVE OF OFFENSIVE PLAY IS TO SCORE. PLAY IN THE offensive zone pits the active attackers against the reactive defense. Disciplined, systematic defenders attempt to throw up a wall around the goal, and the high-flying, creative offensive players try to break through weak spots in the fortifications. Play in the offensive zone is all about flexibility and inventiveness and creating the conditions for effective improvisation.

"Scoring in hockey demands technique plus.... A game that ends 0:0 will not, I believe, be very interesting to watch. No matter how exciting a game may be from the point of view of tactics or technique, it will not be interesting if the tactics do not result in a goal being scored," wrote Anatoli Tarasov in *The Road to Olympus*.

It may seem like an obvious warning, but it is a good point nonetheless; it is possible to overplan a game of hockey, and coaches need to remember that no technique ensures a goal every time the team skates down the ice. Good offensive zone preparation is about unleashing your attackers on the opponents' goal in a way that maximizes the chances of seizing opportunities.

Offensive systems provide general guidelines to assist the team in its tactical preparation. After that, the players must be given the freedom to create and innovate.

After the rush (the initial attack), offensive zone systems allow the team to maintain or regain control of the puck and to continue the attack on the goal. Only a low percentage of goals are scored on the rush. More goals are scored after sustained pressure in the opponents' end.

Technical skills—skating, passing, stickhandling and shooting—are important on offense. Drills should be designed to incorporate the development of technical skills into the plan of attack, and drills should simulate game conditions to familiarize the players with the potential situations and the resulting opportunities.

Good offense requires a hungry, sharp-witted, tireless, clever approach to the game.

POSITIONAL PLAY

The Positional Play system is conservative. Its principles are basic to all offensive play. It teaches the forwards to go to the net, to attack the net. One forward is always thinking defensively, and the attack is always a controlled one because one forward has that defensive responsibility. All systems utilize the basic plays described here at various times. In this system, the wings are responsible for their respective sides and rarely cross the ice to the other side. The center is responsible for the middle and can move to either side. This is a good system for young teams and for those with limited skating ability. Again, all teams make use of Positional Play at times, regardless of their system.

KEY POINTS

1. Positional Play is a conservative system of offense. The objectives are basic, which makes it easy to teach.

2. It stresses that one forward always be in the slot, which places him in a position to backcheck.

3. Two forwards attack the net.

4. The roles of the defensemen are conservative, but they do have the freedom to move into the high slot.

5. This system is effective when the play enters the offensive zone.

The two wings stay on the boards and break for the net. The center stays in the slot.

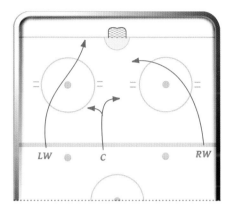

One wing (LW) and the center break for the net. The second wing (RW) moves to the slot.

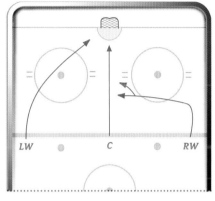

One wing (LW) goes deep in the zone toward the net. Either the second wing (RW) or the center, usually the one who enters the zone last, stays in the slot, and the other can go deep or to the net.

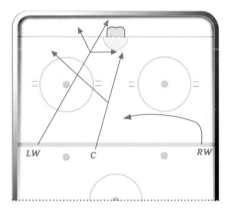

One wing (LW) stays along the boards and goes deep. Either the second wing (RW) or the center, usually the one who enters the zone last, stays in the slot, and the other can go deep or to the net.

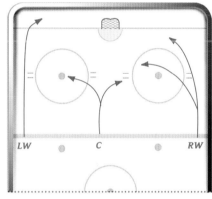

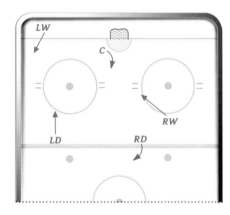

The defensemen are normally conservative and stay on the blue line. They are allowed to move to the high slot when the opportunity arises. When one defenseman (LD) moves in, the second defenseman (RD) moves back a few feet to cover.

DRILLS

To teach this system, specific steps should be taken to familiarize the players with the different situations. It is important that the players know their own and each other's roles. This system depends on the forward with the defensive responsibility. Offensive play must be practiced against opposition some of the time.

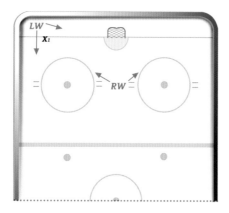

1 Many of the situations that arise during a game call for interactions between two players. Have two forwards practice working together at the different situations. For example, one wing (LW) is deep in the corner with the puck, and the second wing (RW) is in the slot. The two players work the puck toward the net. The opposition can be added, making it a 2-on-1 or 2-on-2 drill.

The different situations **2** involving the three forwards should be practiced. For example, the LW has the puck and carries it deep into the zone. The center goes for the far post, and the RW stays in the slot. The opposition can be added, making it a 3-on-1, 3-on-2 or 3-on-3 drill.

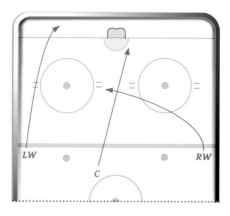

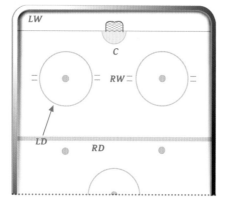

3 The above step with the addition of the defensemen increases the number of offensive situations and therefore the number of possible plays. For example, the LD can move to the top of the circle for a shot on the net. The opposition can be added to create different drills or scrimmage play.

TRIANGULAR OFFENSE

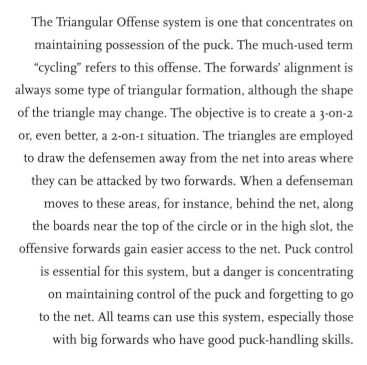

The Triangular Offense system is one that concentrates on maintaining possession of the puck. The much-used term "cycling" refers to this offense. The forwards' alignment is always some type of triangular formation, although the shape of the triangle may change. The objective is to create a 3-on-2 or, even better, a 2-on-1 situation. The triangles are employed to draw the defensemen away from the net into areas where they can be attacked by two forwards. When a defenseman moves to these areas, for instance, behind the net, along the boards near the top of the circle or in the high slot, the offensive forwards gain easier access to the net. Puck control is essential for this system, but a danger is concentrating on maintaining control of the puck and forgetting to go to the net. All teams can use this system, especially those with big forwards who have good puck-handling skills.

KEY POINTS

1. The Triangular Offense should be used when the offensive team has control of the puck and wants to maintain it.

2. The three forwards work in a triangular formation. Their movement is a result of their maneuverability relative to each other, not the movement of the puck. The movement of the puck is a result of the forwards' shifting positions.

3. The objective is to have three forwards isolate on two opposing players. The purpose is to get one forward free to make a play on the net.

4. The roles of the defensemen are conservative, but they do have the freedom to move into the high slot.

5. Puck control and passing are essential.

TRIANGULAR OFFENSE

This formation **1A** has one forward (C) deep along the boards, a second forward (RW) along the boards and the third forward (LW) in the slot

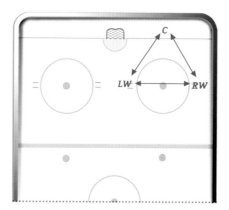

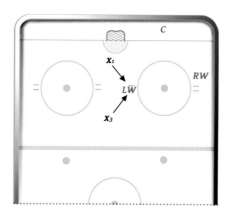

1B The position of the LW makes it difficult for the defenseman (X_1) to cover him. The LW must be covered by the player responsible for the point or the player responsible for the slot. If X_1 moves out, the net area is open; if X_3 moves in, the point is open.

The movement and passwork **1C** of the triangle can put the RW in a position to go to the net or to have an open shot.

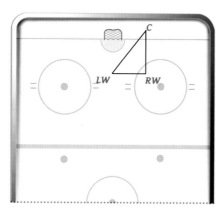

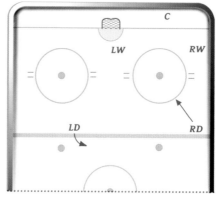

1D The defensemen normally are conservative and stay on the blue line. They are allowed to move to the slot when the opportunity arises. When one defenseman (RD) moves in, the second defenseman (LD) moves back a few feet to cover.

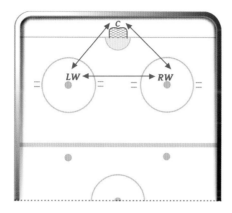

2A This formation has one forward (C) behind the net and the other two forwards (LW and RW) wide in the face-off circles.

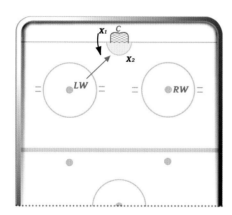

2B The defensive unit has to decide whether to pressure the center or cover the wings. If one defenseman (X1) pressures the center, an avenue may open for one wing to go to the net.

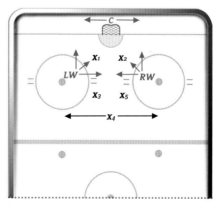

2C If the defensive unit forms a box and attempts to keep the offense to the outside, the three forwards must move short distances in an attempt to make the box move and break down. The triangle is designed to attack any breakdown.

TRIANGULAR OFFENSE

3A This formation has two forwards (LW and C) behind the goal line and the third forward (RW) in the slot.

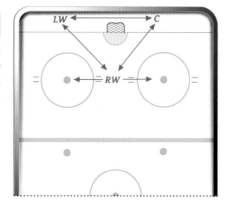

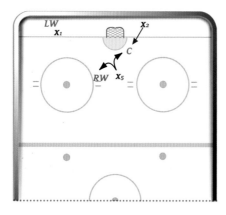

3B The two deep players attempt, through passes, to draw the defensemen away from the net. This will force a forward (X5) to cover the net area.

3C This formation forces the opposition to play many situations man-to-man. If the offensive players are able to win a 1-on-1 situation, they will have a man who is open and moves to the net. In this example, the center has beaten X2, creating a 2-on-1 situation, with X5 forced to cover both the RW and the center.

1 The triangles should be set up. The role for each player should be explained. The players need to know their basic movement patterns and how to move and maintain the triangle.

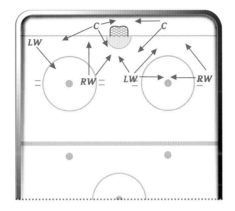

DRILLS

To teach this system, specific steps should be taken to familiarize the players with the different situations. This system is dependent on coordinated movement and passwork. Offensive play must be practiced against opposition some of the time.

2 The triangular movement should be practiced first without pucks. This can be done either with the three forwards or the five-man offensive unit. This teaches the players to move as a reaction to the movement of the others and not as a reaction to the puck. This will be a new idea for many players.

3 Introduce the pucks and practice the triangular movements. This can be done with the three forwards or the five-man offensive unit. Quick passes and short movements are essential. Passing to an open area with a player moving toward it needs to be perfected.

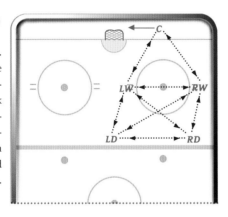

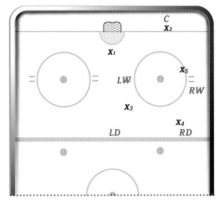

4 Introduce the opposition: first the two defensemen, then one forward followed by the two others. The different drills, such as 3-on-2 and 3-on-3, as well as scrimmage practice are covered by this step.

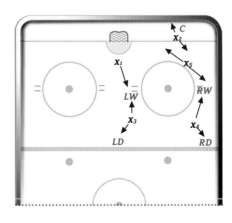

5 Review what the opposition may do to defend against the triangles. It is important for the offensive unit to know where the defensive breakdowns can occur. With this knowledge, the offensive unit will be better prepared to attack. For example, the defensive team players will attempt to restrict the triangle's movement by bringing their wings deeper into the zone. The proper adjustment by the offensive unit is to reestablish the triangle deeper in the zone.

OVERLOAD THE SLOT

The Overload the Slot system of offensive zone play is basic and simple. When the initial rush is unsuccessful and the follow-up attack does not result in a play on the net, the puck is moved to the points. The defensemen's jobs are to shoot the puck and to put it on the net. The forwards' jobs are to go to the net and get in position for tip-ins, deflections and rebounds. One of the objectives is for the forwards to outman the opposing defensemen in front of the net. This is a good system for teams with big forwards. Any forward with the instinct to go to the net will thrive. Courage is an important quality for the forwards to possess. This system, because much of it takes place in front of the net, is a physical one.

KEY POINTS

1. The Overload the Slot system is easy to teach, with objectives that are simple and direct.

2. Pressure is applied to the slot area with two, sometimes three, forwards playing in the slot.

3. The forwards, when in possession of the puck, control it deep. If their attempts to go to the net fail, they will move the puck to the defensemen.

4. The role for the defensemen is simple: Shoot the puck. The forwards move to the slot and net area for tip-ins, deflections and rebounds.

One forward (RW) is in the slot, and a second forward (LW) is deep along the boards. The third forward (C) plays so that he can move to the slot or deep in the zone.

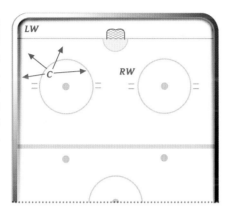

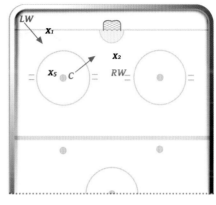

The initial attempt to make the play on the net may have the center go to the net. This will force a defenseman (X2) to cover both the center and the RW if the other defenseman (X1) is on the puck in the corner and if the forward (X5) does not cover the net.

If the LW makes the initial pass to the center, he may head directly to the net. This will crowd the slot area with two offensive and two defensive players.

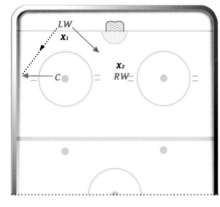

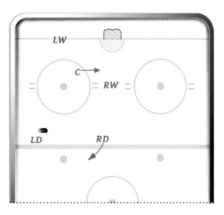

When the puck is moved to the defensemen, they shoot it. The forwards position themselves for tip-ins, deflections and rebounds (Diagrams 2a and 2b).

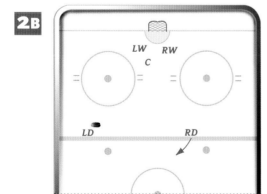

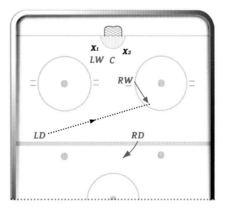

An area that is often open when this system is employed is the top of the far face-off circle. The RW moves to the top of the circle while the other two forwards crowd the slot. In this case, the LD passes, rather than shoots, the puck to the RW.

DRILLS

To teach this system, specific steps should be taken to familiarize the players with the different situations. This system is dependent on the defensemen completing their roles. All offensive play must be practiced against opposition some of the time.

The role of each player should be **1** explained. The players need to know the basic movement patterns and each player's role and understand the particular importance of moving the puck to the points.

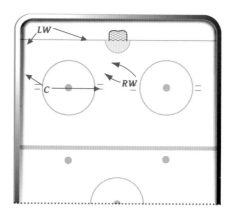

The three forwards work on their basic **2** movement patterns without pucks. The five-man unit works on the basic movement patterns as well. Among other things, this teaches the players to go to the net.

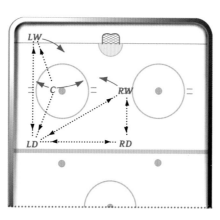

3 Introduce the puck first with the entire five-man unit.

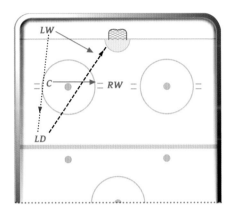

4 A shooting drill with the forwards moving into the slot area for tip-ins, deflections and rebounds teaches the unit quick execution. Stationary objects, such as chairs or traffic cones, can be used to simulate the opposition's defensemen.

The opposition is inserted. **5** The two defensemen are first, then one forward followed by the other two. The different drills, such as 3-on-2 and 3-on-3, as well as scrimmage practice are covered by this step.

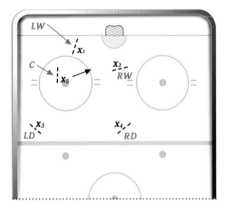

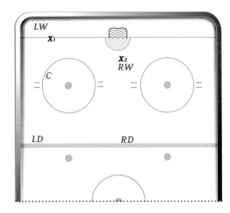

6 Review what the opposition may do to defend against this system. It is important that the offensive unit recognizes the defensive setup in order to prevent the system's major risk—the three forwards being trapped—from happening. Wings will check defensemen closer. All three forwards go to the net.

SPECIAL TEAMS PLAY

THE RULES OF THE GAME MAKE "SPECIAL SITUATIONS" A CRUCIAL PART of hockey. Play moves quickly, penalties are assessed regularly, and they often play an important part in determining the winners and losers. When one team has a player advantage, the other has a player disadvantage. Every power play must be met with penalty killing, and a team that can dominate in these special circumstances usually has a good chance of winning.

The same applies to face-offs. Every time the play stops, there is an opportunity to grab the tempo away from the opposition and to move onto the offensive.

No coach can afford to ignore these situations. Practices must include enough time to cover them, because when you count up the number of times they occur during a game, the importance of preparing for face-offs and penalties becomes obvious.

The game of hockey has room for specialists. Every team can use a centerman with enough quickness and hand-eye coordination to win a high percentage of his draws. A player with limited offensive skills but with a sound understanding of the game can become an excellent penalty killer. A player with quick hands but with little aptitude for physical play can become a goal scorer in those open-ice power play situations.

Not only are coaches wise to emphasize player specialization, but doing so is a gratifying part of the job. All players want to contribute to their team's success, and having a special skill recognized and put to use makes any player happy.

*It is the sum total of the entire unit that counts,
not the total of any one part. I must be patient
first in my evaluation and then in my selection.*

John Wooden
They Call Me Coach

POWER PLAYS

THE IMPORTANCE OF THE POWER PLAY HAS GROWN IN RECENT YEARS, and successful teams are usually ranked among the clubs with the best man-advantage records. Power play opportunities cannot be consistently squandered if a team is to succeed.

Proper coaching is critical for the power play. Sure, it helps to have skilled players, but it still comes down to teamwork and execution. Enough practice time is needed to perfect the power play; all teams should work on the power play at most practices. This usually takes place with one coach and a few players. The other players are working on something else with the other coaches in the other zones.

Power plays are not complicated or complex; in fact, the opposite is true. They are simple, designed to concentrate on two or three areas. Only a few options exist for any power play, and it is the execution that is vital. Power plays start with a 5-on-4 situation. The objective is to eliminate the penalty killers; in essence, to go from a 5-on-4 to a 3-on-2 to a 2-on-1 to a 1-on-0.

Power play personnel are a key to success. There must be a comfortable fit between the personnel and the type of power play used, and it is important for the coach to know his players and their abilities when selecting a power play. Usually, the players with the better skills are on the power play; however, there are enough different power plays to accommodate different styles of players or combinations of the different styles.

Nine power plays are presented here. The first three, the Funnel, the 2-1-2 and the Defensemen Slide, include a suggested step-by-step teaching approach. The coach needs to understand the options for each power play to be able to decide if he has the right players to do the job.

THE FUNNEL

The Funnel power play is a conservative one with limited options. The primary play is to have the defensemen shoot the puck and have the forwards in position for tip-ins, deflections and rebounds. A second option has a forward move away from the net into a face-off circle for a pass. This power play favors big players with the knack for scoring from close range. The forwards must have the courage to play in front of the net and take a pounding.

KEY POINTS

1. The Funnel is a simple power play with limited options available.

2. The objective is to have the defensemen shoot and the three forwards outman the opposition's defensemen for position in front of the net.

3. When entering the offensive zone, the power play should be set up deep in the zone. The initial passes are made to open the points prior to moving the puck to the defensemen.

The power play takes place in a funnel-shaped area. It goes from the points at the boards to the goal posts.

1

2 **Proper Alignment.** The three forwards are in the slot, and the defensemen play normal positions on the blue line.

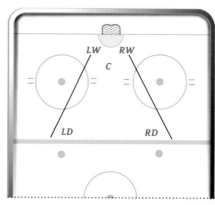

Basic Alignment. When the puck is on the boards, the LD has the puck and the RW moves out away from the net.

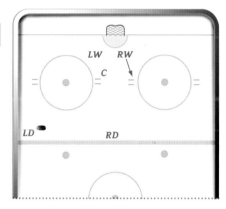

This power play works because the defensemen are usually open at the point to initiate a new move or shot to the net. For example, if one forward (LW) has the puck and he cannot get it to the other two forwards (C and RW), he can look to the defensemen.

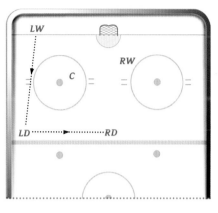

When the puck moves to the defensemen, the three forwards move to the front of the net. The opposition's defensemen will then be outmanned 3-on-2. The forwards must be in position for tip-ins, deflections and rebounds.

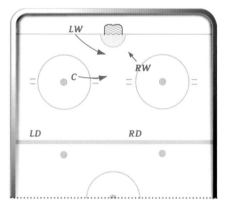

A second play has the LD with the puck along the boards. The off-wing (RW) moves away from the net area into the face-off circle, which creates a passing option.

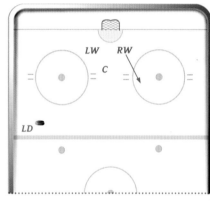

This power play normally emphasizes direct shots on the net, but the RW, by moving away from the net and the penalty killers, becomes open. The LD passes to the RW in the opposite face-off circle.

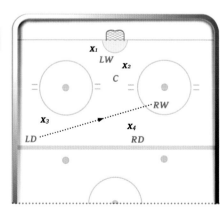

The RW can shoot, which is the high-percentage play, or he can pass to the LW or center, who may be open as a result of the opposition's reaction to the LD's pass.

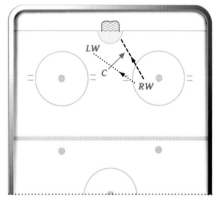

2-1-2

The 2-1-2 power play has great flexibility. The options can emphasize the forwards or the defensemen or both. It can set up deep in the zone, along the blue line or from the boards. The ultimate option is to get the puck to the man in the slot, the "1" man in the 2-1-2 alignment. Another option has the forwards concentrate on the two defensemen. Another is to have the defensemen shoot the puck (similar to the funnel). Passwork is the important skill for this power play. A team needs to have players with effective passing and stickhandling skills to use this power play.

KEY POINTS

1. The 2-1-2 is a balanced power play that works from either the front "2" (forwards) or the back "2" (defensemen).

2. The objective is to get the puck to the man in the slot, who can make a play on the net.

3. There are numerous options available in this power play.

4. When entering the offensive zone, the power play should be set up deep in the zone.

Proper Alignment. **1** Two forwards (LW and RW) are deep in the zone, and one forward (C) is in the slot. The defensemen play normal positions on the blue line.

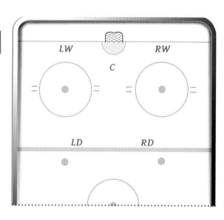

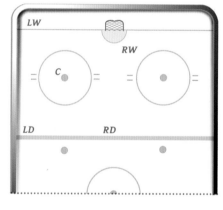

2 If the play shifts to the boards, a similar alignment is used. The 2-1-2 formation remains constant.

The three forwards have **3** room to move without altering the basic alignment. The deep forwards have more freedom to move and redirect the power play than does the forward in the slot.

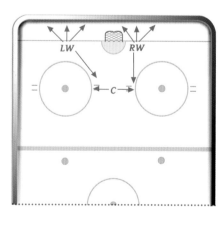

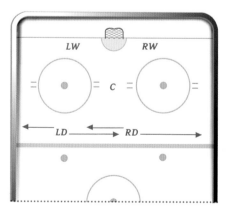

4 The defensemen (LD and RD) can move along the blue line, and the forwards must adjust.

The LD and **5** the RD can pass between each other. The two deep forwards (LW and RW) can move about to create openings.

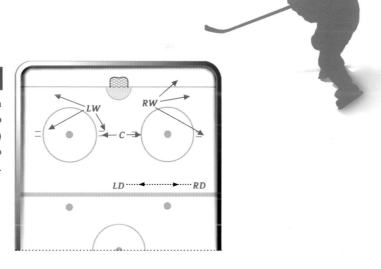

The primary **6** objective of this power play is to get the puck to the man in the slot. The basic passing patterns involve one defenseman (LD), one deep forward (LW) and the forward in the slot (C).

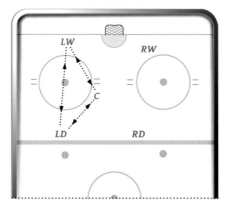

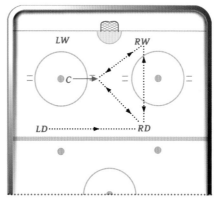

The same play **7** can be executed from the other side when the puck is passed to the RD. The center just has to move a couple of strides across the slot.

The RW is in a **8** position that allows the LD to pass directly to him if the penalty-killing unit plays too loose. If this is done, it creates a 3-on-2 situation. The three forwards can then attack the net.

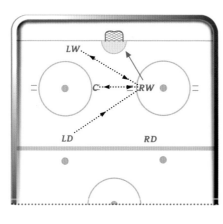

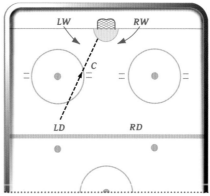

The defensemen **9** have the option of shooting the puck. The three forwards are in positions that allow them to quickly converge on the net for tip-ins, deflections and rebounds.

WINGS PLAY THE OFF-SIDE

The Wings Play the Off-Side power play focuses on the alignment of the players. For instance, the LW is a right shot, and the RW is a left shot. The wings see more of the ice, have better passing angles and can "one-touch" shoot the puck with this alignment. The positioning has the wings spread wide, with the center down deep in the zone. The first option is to move the puck to the wings, who shoot. The center's role is primarily that of a playmaker. Teams that use this power play must have forwards who can one-touch shoot the puck.

1. The Wings Play the Off-Side.

2. The primary objective of this power play is to get the wings open for a shot.

3. The center is primarily a playmaker. He plays deep in the zone and is able to move to the net quickly.

4. The defensemen are secondary shooters.

5. When entering the offensive zone, the puck should be set up on the "strong side"; that is, the side containing three offensive players.

Basic Alignment. The wings (LW and RW) are spread apart. The center is deep in the zone, and the defensemen (RD and LD) play normal positions.

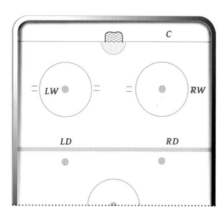

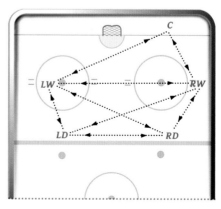

The alignment of the players permits a number of different passing avenues.

3 Player movement on the weak side (LW and LD), coupled with puck movement on the strong side (RW, C and RD), is the key to creating an open man for a shot.

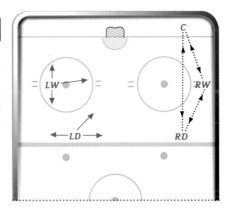

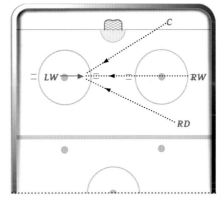

4A **Play 1.** The primary play is to get the LW open for a shot. Normally, this is done with a pass from the strong side (RW, C or RD).

4B In order for the LW to be open, the penalty killer (X3) has to be forced out of position.

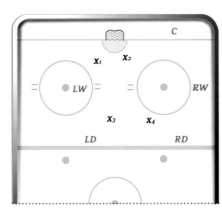

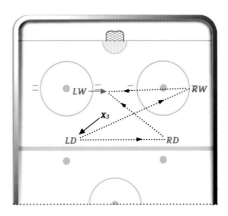

4C This is best done when the LD passes quickly to the RW or the RD, who, in turn, passes to the LW. The LW moves to the slot area before X3 can get back to cover.

Play 2. **5** A second play is to have the RW shift if the penalty killer X4 is out of position. X4's bad positioning (crowding the RD too closely) allows the RW to move to the slot and receive a pass from the LD, the LW or the center.

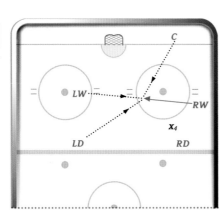

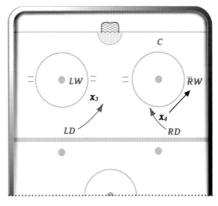

6 **Play 3.** A third possible play is to have a defenseman (LD) move into a position to shoot. Then if X3 checks the LD too closely or if X4 checks the RW too closely, the defenseman (RD) is able to move to a high-percentage shot area.

1 - 2 - 2

The 1-2-2 power play focuses on the alignment of the players. The initial alignment, with the wings wide and the center deep, utilizes most of the offensive zone. The three forwards are spread farther apart than in the Wings Play the Off-Side power play. The purpose of this alignment is to force the defensive unit to spread out. The options are determined by the penalty-killing unit. If the penalty-killing box stays tight, the power play moves the puck around the outside for a shot. If the box spreads out, the power play will go down deep in the zone and attack the two defensemen. To make either option work, this power play must have players who can pass the puck as well as carry it while moving around small areas.

KEY POINTS

1. The 1-2-2 power play utilizes much of the offensive zone with its spread-out alignment.

2. The center usually plays the deep position and is able to quarterback the play from there.

3. The wings play spread out.

4. The defensemen play a spread-out position.

5. The tactical approach is flexible. The power play unit reacts to the penalty killers' alignment.

6. When entering the offensive zone, the puck should be set up deep in the zone.

Proper Alignment. **1**
The center is deep near the net. The wings (LW and RW) are spread far apart, and the defensemen (LD and RD) play a wide position. With each play, the formation collapses toward the front of the net. If the play on the net is unsuccessful, the formation opens out again.

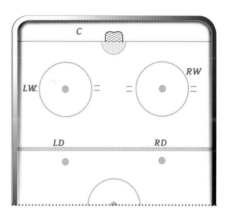

The forwards **2**
have a number of possible movements they can make without changing the basic alignment.

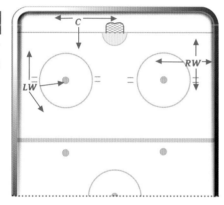

3 If penalty killers use a wide box to defend against the 1-2-2, the normal tactic will be to keep the puck deep, with the forwards (LW, C and RW) attacking X_1 and X_2.

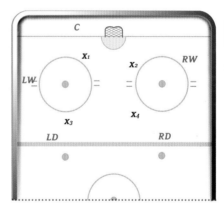

FROM THE CORNER

The From the Corner power play focuses on its place of origin, the corner. The options are directed from the corner, and the power play unit initially sets up with the puck in the corner. Whenever it needs to regain positional control, one player controls the puck in the corner. The primary option is to keep the puck deep and attack the defensemen. A second option is to get the puck to the points if one of the penalty-killing forwards moves in deep to help his defensemen. Teams that use this power play must have at least two forwards who are capable of controlling the puck deep in the corner and quarterbacking it from there.

KEY POINTS

1. The From the Corner power play originates in the corner and plays aggressively deep for the most part.

2. One forward is responsible for setting up in the corner to start the play. This is done with the belief that the opposition will not break the box to go into the corner.

3. The other forwards have freedom to move about.

4. The defensemen play normal positions, but either may move onto the offensive.

5. The primary objective is always to play 3-on-2 against the penalty-killing unit's two defensemen and, if possible, to slide a defenseman deep to create a 4-on-2 situation.

Proper Alignment. **1**
One forward (LW) sets up in the corner with the puck, and the other two forwards (RW and C) play normal positions, with freedom to move about. The defensemen (LD and RD) play normal positions. The direction of the power play is always from the corner and to the net or slot area. For the most part, the puck remains deep in the zone.

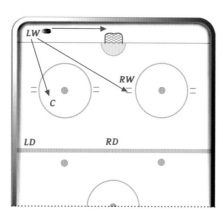

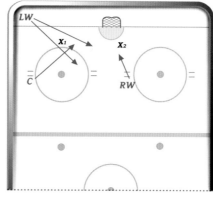

2 This power play puts constant pressure on the opposition's defensemen (X1 and X2).

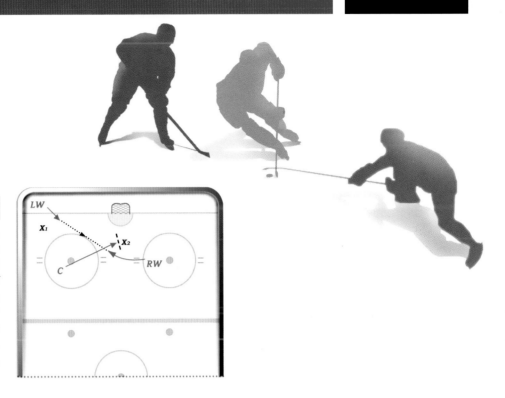

Play 1.

The simplest play is for the three forwards to attack X1 and X2. For example, the center moves to the net, the RW moves across the slot, and the LW, with the puck, moves out of the corner. The center attempts to screen X2, and the LW and the RW attack X1 (who will have moved to the front of the net) in a 2-on-1 situation. Ideally, the RW has a play on net.

Play 2.

A second play has the LW in the corner with the puck. The RW goes behind the net for a pass, and the center moves either to the net or to the slot area. The LD slides into the area at the top of the face-off circle.

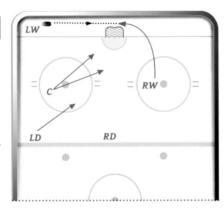

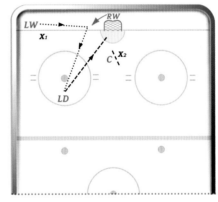

4B The resulting play could be a pass from the LW to the RW, who, in turn, passes to the LD, who is open for a shot.

Play 3.

Another play has the center move to the net. The RW moves into the slot, and the RD moves to the top of the face-off circle. The LD moves to the middle of the blue line to cover, and the LW has the puck in the corner.

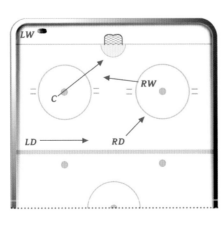

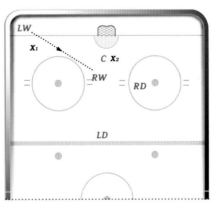

5B The initial play could be for the LW to pass to the RW in the slot. This would put three players (RW, C and RD) against X2.

DIAMOND FORMATION

The Diamond Formation power play has a 2-2-1 alignment, with a defenseman as the "1." The primary option is to have the "1" shoot the puck and the deeper twosome go to the net. Passing is the critical skill for this power play. The players, once in this alignment, have limited room to move around. It is the passwork that forces the penalty-killing unit to get out of position and free up the "1" for the shot. This power play is a good option to work within many of the other power plays. Teams must have players who can pass the puck for this power play.

KEY POINTS

1. The 2-2-1 formation comprises two sets of forwards and one defenseman.

2. Passwork is important for the success of this power play.

3. The four forwards are all primary shooters when they become open.

4. The defenseman can be a shooter but is more often a playmaker.

5. This power play is balanced. It can work from either the right or the left side.

Proper Alignment. **1** Two forwards (LW and C) are deep. The third forward (RW) and a defenseman (LD) are the second pair and are near or in the face-off circles. The RD is the only defenseman on the blue line.

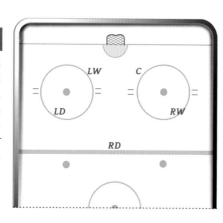

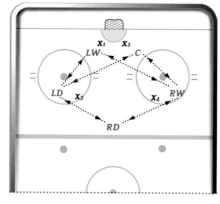

2 The opposition usually counters with a wide box that plays the four players in the zone man-to-man. The RD is therefore often left alone in the middle of the blue line. There are a number of passing avenues.

Play 1.
The RD has the puck. He may shoot, though it is a low-percentage shot. If a penalty killer (X4) moves to him, he passes to the RW.

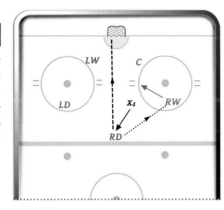

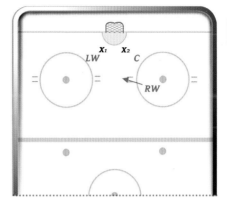

3B The RW moves to the net in a 3-on-2 situation with the LW and center.

Play 2.
A second play has the RD, the LD and the LW passing on one side. If neither the LW nor the LD is able to get to the net, the RW can move to the slot for a pass from the LW.

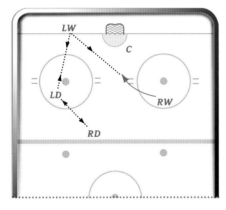

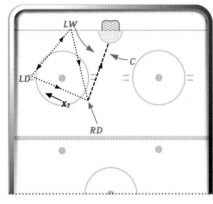

4B Another option has the LD moving back toward the board, drawing X3 with him. This permits the RD to move into the high slot for a pass from the LD. The RD now has a high-percentage shot if he chooses to shoot.

Play 3.
A third play has the two deep forwards (LW and C) move behind the goal line. This usually forces the penalty killers' box to move in farther. The RD can move in off the blue line for a pass from either the LD or the RW.

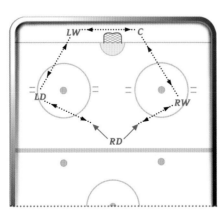

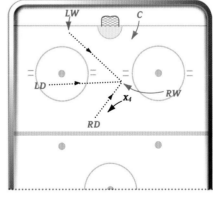

5B Often a penalty killer (X4) moves to the RD. The RW becomes open and can move into the slot. The RW can take a pass from the RD, the LD or the LW.

*All players want to contribute
to their team's success, and having
a special skill recognized and put to use
makes any player happy.*

Michael A. Smith

PENALTY KILLING

A TEAM'S ABILITY TO KILL OFF PENALTIES IS EVERY BIT AS IMPORTANT as its ability to score when it is on the power play. Yet when special situations are considered, coaches too often place all the emphasis on power play skills. Effective penalty killing negates the opposition's best scoring opportunities and enables your team to return to even strength full of confidence. The ideal is to have good power play skills *and* sound penalty killing; teams with both will usually be successful.

Penalty killing is an extension of a team's defensive play. Whether aggressive, conservative or a combination of both, a team's defensive style should be reflected in its penalty-killing tactics. A team with good speed can attack the puck in the offensive zone, while a team that has size is more likely to stress disciplined play in its own end. As in all other systems, the abilities of team personnel decide how the coach should proceed.

Penalty killing, even more than normal defense, is a matter of reacting to the puck and the offensive team's alignment. Yes, the defensive strategy is important, and teams must have penalty-killing plans, but more than anything else, capable penalty killing requires quick, intelligent reaction.

In the offensive zone, the penalty-killing units have some room for creativity and aggressive pursuit, but as the play moves into the neutral zone, the checking becomes closer and more methodical. With fewer defenders available, it becomes all the more crucial that the offense not be given opportunities to capitalize on a defender's mistake. In the defensive zone, the focus is on disciplined play intended either to gain possession of the puck or simply to clear the zone. A coach must constantly remind penalty killers that possession does not need to result in an effective breakout. Players must never hesitate to ice the puck.

It is difficult to practice killing penalties. Certainly, one way to do so is in a scrimmage situation against the power play unit. In general, however, this is an area that relies on the coach's ability to communicate ideas.

1-3

KEY POINTS

The 1-3 system combines conservatism with aggressiveness. In the offensive zone, one forward forechecks and pressures the puck while a second stays back toward the blue line. If the forechecking forward is successful in pressuring the puck, the second forward can become aggressive and join in the pressure. If the forechecking forward is not successful, the second forward is able to move to the neutral zone and assist the defensemen. This prevents any 3-on-2 or 4-on-2 breaks. In the neutral zone, the conservative forward can pressure the puck, clog up the middle or shut down one of the outside lanes. A team needs to have some fast-skating forwards to use this system. A team with size and some skating ability can use this as well.

1. The 1-3 system combines conservatism with the aggressive forechecking of one forward.

2. One forward pressures the puck, and the second forward stays back to prevent 3-on-2 breakouts. The second forward can move in if the first forward successfully pressures the puck.

3. In this system, the wings normally cover the outside lanes, and the defense covers the middle in the neutral zone. This system, however, allows some flexibility for the forwards.

Basic Alignment. **1**
One forward (P1) is deep, and the second forward (P2) stays back toward the blue line. The defensemen play their normal positions on the opponents' blue line.

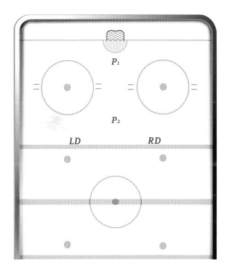

2 The forwards each cover one side of the ice. If P1 goes with the puck, P2 moves to the side away from the puck. The reverse can be used, with P2 moving to the puck and P1 moving to the opposite side. The positioning of P2 should discourage the power play unit from coming up the middle.

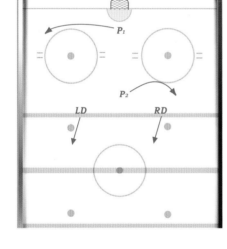

In the neutral zone, the forwards **3A** cover the outside lanes. The defensemen are responsible for the middle and should stand up and force the play.

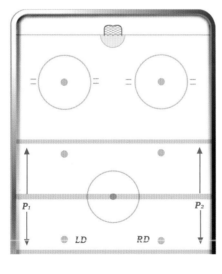

3B In the neutral zone, P2 clogs up the middle, with the objective of forcing the play toward the boards. P1, if he can get back, has the choice of moving to one side or the other. The defensemen play wide and are responsible for the outside lanes. A variation of this is to have P2 pressure the puck when it is in the middle of the ice.

2-2

The 2-2 is an aggressive system. It attacks the power play in the offensive zone, with the purpose of keeping it bottled up. The objective is to prevent the power play from setting up in its own end and breaking out. The two forwards exert steady pressure on the puck. They are constantly skating. Both forwards must be cognizant of their responsibility to move quickly to the defensive if the power play clears the zone. In the neutral zone, the first forward back takes an outside lane while the second comes back through the middle. Skating ability, speed and quickness are essential for this system because the attacking forwards must be able to recover immediately if the need arises. Teams without these skills cannot use it.

1. The 2-2 is an aggressive system that pressures the power play unit constantly in the offensive zone.

2. One forward goes deep to force the puck, and the other forward stays in the high slot.

3. This system demands good skating ability and hard work from the forwards.

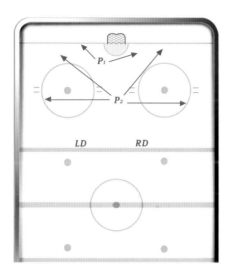

1   **Basic Alignment.**
The first forward (P1) goes deep in the zone to pressure the puck. The second forward (P2) stays in the high slot. P2 is skating and is in a position to move in on the puck or to come back along either side. The defensemen (LD and RD) play their normal positions on the blue line.

The forwards can come down the **2A** boards or the middle. The objective is to have both forwards skating and able to pressure the puck. The second forward (P2) has to anticipate the reaction to the initial pressure of P1 to determine his action (Diagrams 2a and 2b).

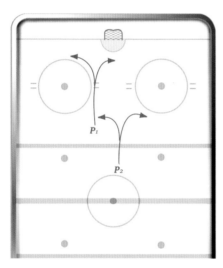

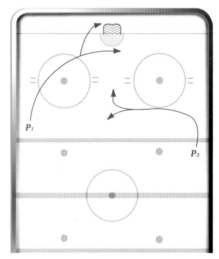

2B

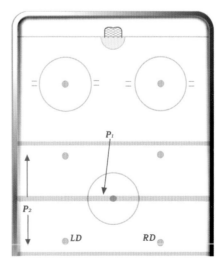

3 In the neutral zone, the first forward back (P2) takes one side. The two defensemen cover the rest of the ice. The second forward (P1), who is usually late because he was forechecking deep, comes back down the middle.

WIDE BOX

The Wide Box is a system that combines conservatism with aggressive play. Its objective is to discourage the opposition's defensemen from playing a prominent role in the power play. It covers a large segment of the offensive zone. The players need to have good mobility so that they can prevent the power play from moving to the inside of the box (slot area) and constantly confront the puck. The alignment is conservative; the aggressiveness comes with its mobility. All teams can use this system.

KEY POINTS

1. The Wide Box is a system that attempts to cover a large portion of the offensive zone with its box. The players require good mobility.

2. The objective is to take the points away from the power play. It attempts to eliminate shots from the points and to encourage the defensemen to pass the puck back to the forwards.

3. The defensemen are responsible for covering the slot.

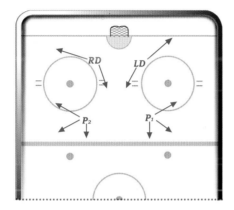

1A **Basic Alignment.** The four penalty killers form a wide box. The box attempts to cover a large section of the offensive zone. The forwards (P1 and P2) can go as far out as the blue line and as wide as the boards. The defensemen (LD and RD) can go out into the slot and as wide as the boards.

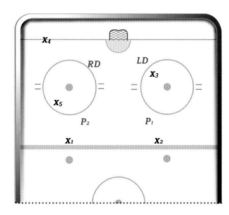

1B The Wide Box discourages the power play from using the points.

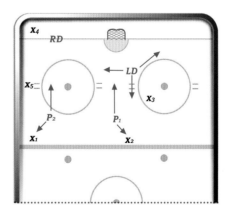

1C It is the responsibility of the forwards (P1 and P2) to cover the points and also to cover the high slot. The defenseman away from the puck (LD) has to cover the slot.

MOVABLE BOX

The Movable Box is an aggressive system. It was primarily utilized first by the Czech national teams of the 1970s and 1980s. Its objective is to attack at every position—to attack the puck at all times. It tries to prevent the power play from setting the tempo and forces the power play unit to make plays before they are properly set up. Anticipation is the essence of this system. If one player attacks the puck, the others must cover for him and anticipate where the puck will go. Then they attack the puck there. Skating ability is crucial as well. The ability to play physically is also important.

KEY POINTS

1. The Movable Box is an aggressive system, with the penalty killers constantly moving and pressuring the puck. It attempts to pressure the players of the power play unit into moving the puck before they are ready.

2. The objective is to attack the puck and control the power play unit. It does not allow the power play to set the tempo.

3. It covers all areas: the points, slot, corners and boards. The constant motion and pressure demands coordinated movement.

Basic Alignment. 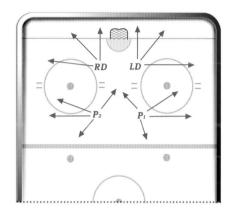 The four penalty killers form a moderate box. The box moves and goes to the puck. All four players have great liberty in their movement patterns.

The Movable Box attacks the puck. When one player moves, the others move as well. For instance, if the defenseman (RD) goes to the puck (X4), one of the forwards (P2) moves to cover a possible outlet (X5) and the other forward (P1) drops into the slot.

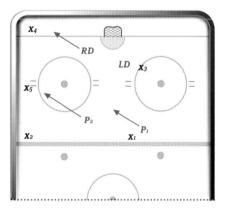

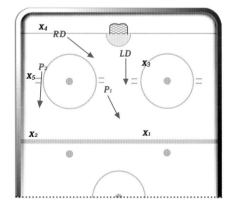

When the puck is moved (in this instance, to the point, X2), all the penalty killers have to react. P2 moves to the point, P1 moves to the other point (X1), the LD moves out into the slot, and the RD moves back to his initial position. Anticipation is needed to shut down the passing routes.

PLANNING & ORGANIZATION FOR THE SEASON

A PREREQUISITE TO EVERY ASPECT OF COACHING IS PROPER PLANNING. Team success, which usually reflects coaching success, is dependent on the use of organizational skills. Poor organizational skills hinder the coaching process as well as the development of the team. Sound coaching techniques begin with planning and organization.

There are three kinds of questions every coach must consider when he sits down to make his plan for the season. The first concerns the different elements of coaching, such as the team roster, game schedules and the practice calendar, which must include time for conditioning, skills training and tactical and systems training. How are the elements related? Is there a priority for the elements? Is the coach especially strong in one area? Do the priorities change during the season? As a coach, you'll have to give serious thought to these needs through good sound planning.

The second set of questions focuses on the team. What is the level of competition? How successful was the team last year? What are the team's strengths and weaknesses? What are the team's goals for this year? What style of play will the team use? Which systems will be utilized? Which drills will be needed to complement the style of play and systems? The questions again are numerous but must be considered when implementing a season's plan.

The final questions concern the individual players on the team. What is the skill level of the players? What are the strengths and weaknesses of the individual players? What skills are needed for the planned style of play and systems? Does the team have good leaders among its players? From which players do you anticipate problems?

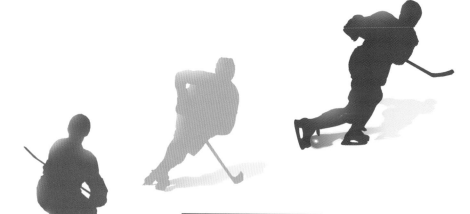

What can be done to prevent or alleviate them? Proper time and attention should be given to dealing with the individual players, both as a group and individually. A season's plan needs to provide the essential time to attend to the individual players.

This chapter will provide an example of a season-long coaching plan. It will include goals for the seasons, types of practices to be used, tactical plans for the team, a season-long conditioning plan, time for coach-player meetings and provisions to alter the plan if the team is not meeting anticipated levels.

Everything the coach does during the season is based on the season's plan. A good plan helps to eliminate or control the problems that inevitably arise. The plan serves as a reference point during the season. This is particularly useful when things are not going well. A plan that has been implemented with proper thought and detail prevents impromptu changes. It is precisely the constant occurrence of these problems and situations that warrants a plan.

DESCRIPTION OF TEAM: The team has an 18-player roster in a league comprising 15- and 16-year-old players. It is anticipated that 12 to 14 players will be 16 years old, with the remainder being 15. Between 10 and 12 players will have played last year. Last year's record was 14-17-5, with a play-off record of 1-2-0. The league has nine other teams. Each team plays every other team four times during the season, twice at home and twice away. The longest trip is approximately 75 minutes by car. The schedule calls for two games a week, on Wednesdays and Saturdays. Normally, there will be one home and one away game each week. The team has practice time

twice a week: on Mondays and Fridays for 60 minutes. The team has two coaches, who are both back for a second year.

League rules permit two weeks of four practices each prior to the start of the season. The league mandates that each team must have two weeks of off-ice training prior to the start of on-ice practices.

Six teams make the play-offs. The top two finishing clubs receive byes in the first round. Each round consists of a best-of-three schedule. The championship round is the best of five.

A general preview of the players indicates that the players' ability level will not be significantly different from last year. There are not likely to be any dominating players, although there will be a consistent level of skill throughout the club. The skill level is adequate. With 10 to 12 players returning, the team will be more experienced than last year's. The team is not especially quick but has enough size to compensate for what it lacks in overall team quickness. The goaltending should be strong, with a returning 16-year-old whose record last year was 9-8-1. The second goalie will be one of two 15-year-olds whose records were 17-3-5 and 11-5-4 on last year's team of 14-year-olds.

The coaches' strengths are in skill development and conditioning. Their tactical approach will lean toward conservative, stressing strong positional play. They are not confident or comfortable playing an aggressive, wide-open style of hockey. They anticipate introducing a second system of forechecking and power play by midseason. The team's strength, however, will be mastering the systems used by last year's team. The major priority for the coaches is to develop the individual skills and the team concept. A .500 season in a competitive league would be considered an excellent year.

THE PLAN

TEAM GUIDELINES

Goals

1. Improvement in skills area.
2. Improvement in the team concept.
3. Maintain a high level of conditioning.
4. A .500 season.

1. Practices will include tactical, conditioning and skill drills.

2. Every practice will end with a fun competitive drill.

3. The team will begin the season with a 1-2-2 forechecking system and comparable systems for the other zones.

4. The team will use three types of practices during the season.

SEASON CALENDAR

Practices

Preseason: 75 minutes

Type 1 (PS1)
30% skills
30% tactical
25% conditioning
15% fun competition

Type 2 (PS2)
40% tactical
25% skills
25% conditioning
10% fun competition

Season: 60 minutes

Type 1 (P1)
50% tactical
20% skills
20% conditioning
10% fun competition

Type 2 (P2)
50% skills
20% tactical
20% conditioning
10% fun competition

Type 3 (P3)
30% skills
30% tactical
30% conditioning
10% fun competition

Games (G)

Week	Monday	Wednesday	Friday	Saturday
1 (pre-season)	PS2	PS1	PS1	PS2
2 (pre-season)	PS2	PS1	PS2	PS1
3	P1	G	P3	G
4	P2	G	P1	G
5	P1	G	P2	G
6	P2	G	P3	G
7	P1	G	P2	G
8	P2	G	P3	G
9	P1	G	P2	G
10	P1	G	P3	G
11	P3	G	P1	G
12	P1	G	P2	G
13	P2	G	P3	G
14	P1	G	P2	G
15	P3	G	P2	G
16	P3	G	P3	G
17	P2	G	P1	G
18	P2	G	P1	G
19	P1	G	P2	G
20	P2	G	P3	G

Notes:

—Much of the tactical time will be spent on drills that emphasize team play, such as breakouts, power plays, forechecking, neutral-zone counter-attacks, etc.

—Every practice will end with a competition-type drill, such as showdowns, relay races, etc.

—Emphasis will be on the team developing puck-control skills.

—Time tests will periodically be used to evaluate improvements in quickness, agility, passing and puckhandling.

—Players will be given a calisthenics program to do on their own at home.

—Some new systems will be introduced near the mid-season mark. For weeks 8, 9 and 10, practices will place more time and emphasis on tactics.

—Coaches will meet with individual players during weeks 3 and 4, 11 and 12, and 17 and 18.

TACTICS

START OF THE YEAR

Forechecking: Basic 1-2-2

Defensive Zone: Zone coverage

Breakouts: Balanced positional play

Neutral Zone: 1-2-2 defensively, positional play offensively

Power Play: Funnel with three forwards in the slot area

Penalty Killing: Basic 1-1-2

MIDSEASON

Forechecking: 1-1-3 encouraging some aggressive play

Power Play: 2-1-2

Penalty Killing: 2-2

1. Early in the year, place emphasis on learning the positional approach to the team play.

2. Drills for passing, puckhandling and shooting will mirror team's systems as often as possible.

3. If team masters the systems introduced early in the year, a few new systems, which encourage aggressiveness with positional play, will be introduced.

4. Early in the year, all the players will practice the special situations (power play and man down) and play in the games. A decision about using special teams will be made at midseason.

OFF-ICE TRAINING

Four different workouts for the two-week period.

1 Mondays:
Warm-ups (15 min.)
Interval running (35 min.)
Run 60 sec./rest 180 sec. 4 times
Run 20 sec./rest 80 sec. 6 times
Run 6 sec./rest 24 sec. 6 times
Hockey-skill circuit (30 min.)
Warm-down (5 min.)

2 Wednesdays:
Warm-ups (15 min.)
Aerobic run (15 min.) 1 $\frac{1}{4}$ to 2 miles
Volleyball (15 min.) Three teams of six
each, rotate teams every three points.
Calisthenics (10 min.)
Hockey-skill circuit (15 min.)
Warm-down (5 min.)

3 Fridays:
Warm-ups (15 min.)
Aerobic run (15 min.) 1 $\frac{1}{4}$ to 2 miles
Soccer game (20 min.) Three teams
of six each, rotate after every goal.
Breakout plays (15 min.) Players go
through team's different breakouts
using volleyball.
Hockey-skill circuit (15 min.)
Warm-down (5 min.)

4 Saturdays:
Warm-ups (15 min.)
Volleyball (20 min.) Three teams of
six each, rotate teams every three points;
Football (20 min.) Three teams of
six each, rotate every four downs;
each team has four downs to go
25 yards to score.
Warm-down (5 min.)

5 Goalies.
Every practice will have
goalie-oriented shooting drills.
An off-ice practice consisting of
agility, mobility and skill drills will
be given to the goalies to do at home.
The goalies will be warmed up
off-ice prior to each practice.
The goalies will know in advance
when they are playing the games.

EXAMPLE PRACTICE 1

TYPE 1 (P1)

0-5 minutes
Warm-Ups. **1**

Light skating, doing turns, spins, falls, etc., with and without pucks.

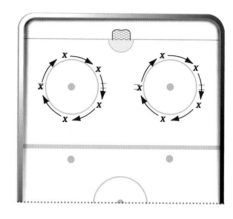

2A **6-15 minutes**
Three Skill Drills.

Three drills, one in each zone: Backward skating on a face-off circle.

Players skate **2B** figure-8s while stickhandling.

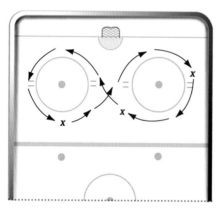

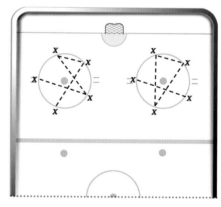

2C Players make passes while standing still on a face-off circle.

16-30 minutes
Breakout Drills. **3A**

Defenseman begins 1-on-1 drill with an outlet pass.

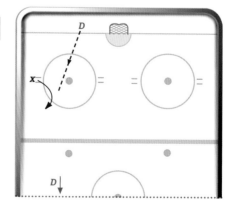

Defenseman
begins 2-on-1
drill with an outlet pass.

3B

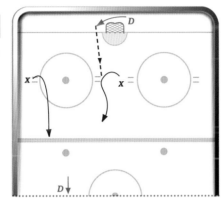

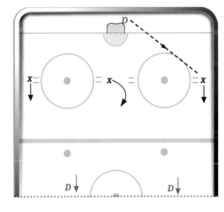

3C

Defenseman
begins 3-on-1
and 3-on-2 drills with
an outlet pass.

**31-35 minutes
Conditioning Drill.** **4**

Players skate 1½ laps,
skate 22 seconds, rest 44
seconds. Three times.

**36-40 minutes
Passing Drill.** **5**

Pairs make one-touch
pass while moving
in one zone. Six
players in each zone.

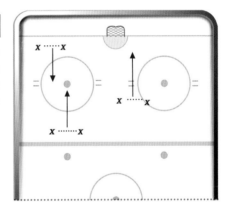

**41-50 minutes
Forechecking.** **6**

Instruction on forechecking
system. Players go through
system and possible adjustments
of the opposition.

**51-55 minutes
Conditioning Drill.** **7**

Players skate hard to the
blue line, turn and come
back to the goal line easy.
Skate 4 seconds and rest 12
seconds. Six to eight times.

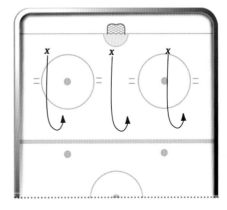

8 **56-60 minutes
Relay Race.**

Teams of four players
each skate down and
back once.

EXAMPLE PRACTICE 2
TYPE 1 (P1)

0-5 minutes **1**
Warm-Ups.
Skating easy, players in groups of three pass the puck between themselves. One player skates backward, two forward.

6-15 minutes **2A**
Two Shooting
Drills. One in each end. Player breaks off wing and shoots.

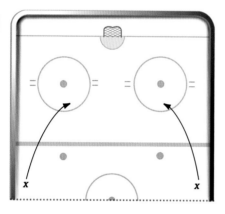

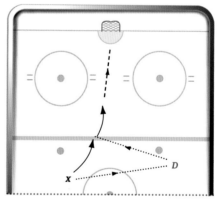

2B Forward passes to defenseman, breaks to the net, receives a return pass and shoots.

16-22 minutes **3**
Defensive-Zone
Coverage. Instruction on defensive-zone coverage.

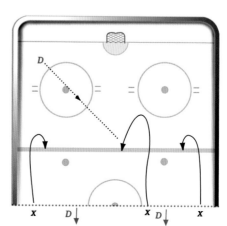

4 **23-28 minutes**
Counterattack.
Three forwards begin 3-on-2 attack with outlet pass from a defenseman. Drill goes both ways.

**29-35 minutes
Conditioning Drill.** **5**

Players skate down and back.
Skate 15 seconds and rest
45 seconds. Five times.

**36-40 minutes
Stickhandling Drill.** **6A**

Players skate laps and
weave around pylons.

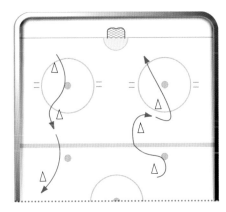

Players skate **6B**
laps and make
circles around pylons.

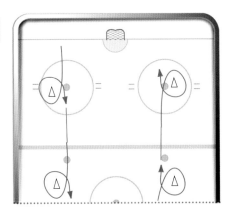

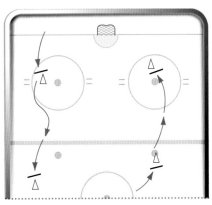

Players **6C**
skate laps
and stop at pylons.

**41-55 minutes
Power Play** **7**
and Penalty Killing.

Instruction and execution
of power-play and man-
down situations.

8 **56-60 minutes
Target Shooting.**

From the blue line, players
try to hit Frisbee that is
hanging from the net.

EXAMPLE PRACTICE 3

TYPE 2 (P2)

1 **0-5 minutes**
Warm-Ups.

Players skate easy in pairs and pass the puck between themselves and then play 1-on-1. Executed while skating laps.

6-10 minutes
Shooting Drill. **2**

Players swing out of the corners and shoot on the goal. Use both ends of the rink.

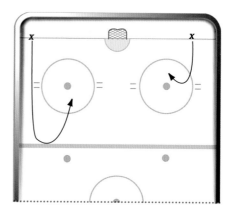

11-20 minutes
Passing Drills. **3A**

Two drills executed on face-off circle. Stationary passing on face-off circle.

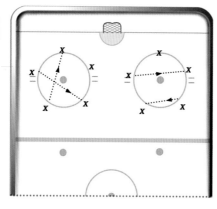

3B Make pass to man ahead while skating around face-off circle.

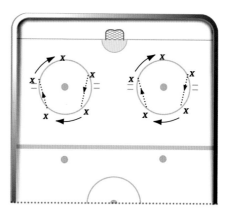

21-27 minutes **4**
Neutral-Zone
Counterattack.
Instruction on the neutral-
zone counterattack.

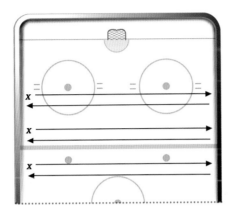

5 **28-35 minutes**
Conditioning Drill.
Skate width of the ice, over and back.
Skate 12 seconds and rest 36 seconds.
Six times.

36-43 minutes **6**
Puckhandling
Drill. Players work on
taking a pass in the feet
and deflecting the puck
to the stick.

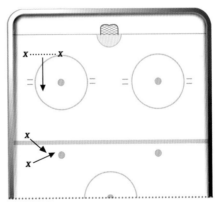

7 **44-50 minutes**
Stickhandling
Drill. Players working in
pairs begin passing the
puck between themselves.
On whistle, they play
1-on-1, trying to keep the
puck to themselves.

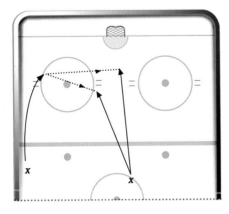

8 **51-55 minutes**
Shooting Drill.
One player moves to
the corner with a puck.
Second player moves to
the slot area and shoots
or deflects pass from
the first player.

9 **56-60 minutes**
Rapid Shooting.
Each player shoots five
pucks quickly from the
red line at the empty goal.
Coaches can keep count
of the number of goals.

EXAMPLE PRACTICE 4
TYPE 2 (P2)

**0-5 minutes
Warm-Ups.** **1**
Start with light, easy skating, and gradually pick up the tempo.

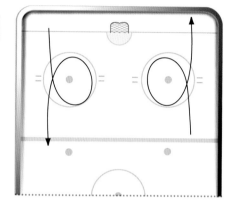

2 **6-10 minutes
Stickhandling
Drill.** Players, in groups of four or five, skate circles at each face-off circle while carrying the puck.

3A **11-25 minutes
Skill Drills.**
Player moves with the puck from the corner toward the net or the slot area to shoot.

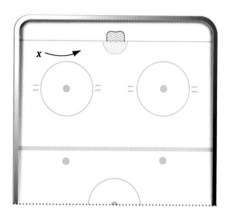

Two players **3B**
skate up-ice making short passes and come back wide, each carrying the puck.

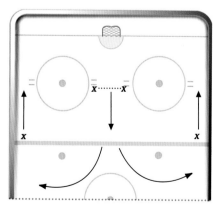

3C The players each have a puck and try to avoid each other while moving in the neutral zone.

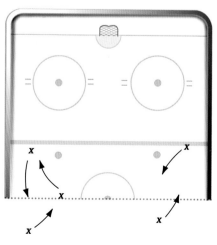

**26-30 minutes
Face-Offs.** **4**

Instruction
on face-offs.

**31-40 minutes
Conditioning Drill.** **5**

In groups of four or five
players, skate two laps.
Skate 30 seconds and rest
90 seconds. Four times.

6 **41-50 minutes
Power Play
and Penalty Killing.**

Using units, practice
both the power-play and
man-down situations.

**51-60 minutes
Games of 3 vs. 3** **7**

Using the width of the ice,
play three separate games
of 3 vs. 3. Emphasize
quick, short passes.

EXAMPLE PRACTICE 5
TYPE 3 (P3)

**0-5 minutes
Warm-Ups.** **1**
Easy skating and stretching.
Skate three laps, each at a
quicker tempo.

**6-15 minutes
Skating Drills.** **2A**
Two drills. Players skate
to the blue line, stop,
then take two or three
quick strides in the
other direction.

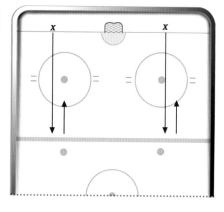

2B Work on
forward and
backward crossovers
while skating on a
face-off circle.

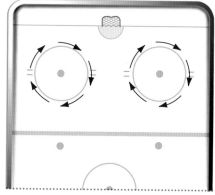

**16-25 minutes
Aerobic Skate.** **3**
Players skate at 60% to
70% maximum speed
continuously in laps.
Skate 3 minutes and rest
1 minute. Two times.

4 **26-40 minutes
Forechecking and
Breakouts.** Working with two
units in each end, practice
forechecking systems and
breakout plays.

**41-50 minutes
Skill Drills.** **5A**

Three drills. Players
work on taking pass
off the boards.

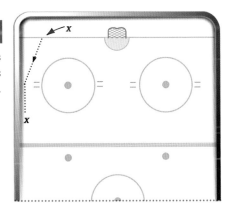

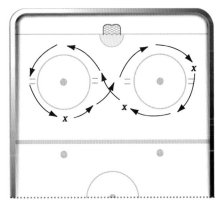

5B Players work
on turns by skating
figure-8s, going hard on
turns and easy
on straightaways.

Shooting drill **5C**
has player receive
a pass as he moves into
slot area and shoots.

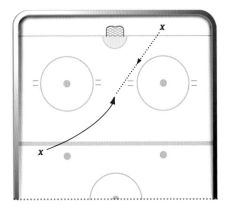

**51-55 minutes
Conditioning Drill.** **6**

Players work short, quick
intervals by skating hard
for 5 seconds and rest
20 seconds while carrying
a puck. Eight times.

7 **56-60 minutes
Showdown.**

EXAMPLE PRACTICE 6
TYPE 3 (P3)

0-5 minutes
Warm-Ups. **1**

Easy skating, with players working in pairs shadowing each other.

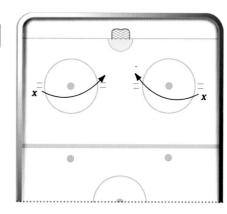

2 **6-10 minutes**
Shooting Drill.

Players come off boards and shoot.

11-20 minutes
Checking. **3A**

Centers and defensemen work on coverage in the net and the slot area.

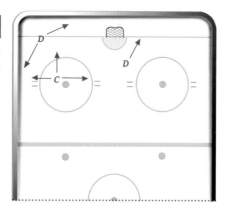

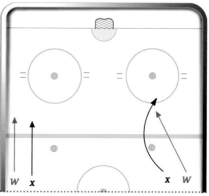

3B Wings work on covering checks while backchecking.

21-35 minutes
Conditioning Drill. **4**

Players skate three laps. Skate 60 seconds and rest 180 seconds. Three times.

**36-45 minutes
Skating Drills.** **5A**

Two skating drills.
Players work on
stepovers.

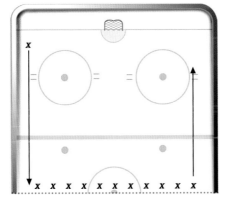

Agility training,
with players moving
in all four directions. **5B**

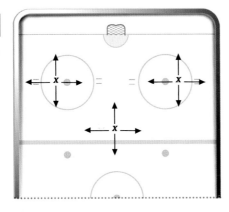

6 **46-50 minutes
Breakout Play.**

Units break out 5-on-2 to
neutral zone, regroup, then
break out a second time.
Work both ends.

**51-55 minutes
Conditioning Drill.** **7**

Players skate between goal line
and blue line continuously.
Skate 15 seconds and rest
45 seconds. Four times.

8 **56-60 minutes
Agility Test.**

Players are timed while
skating an agility course.
(Approximately 20 seconds.)